T0355809

"Every girl I've ever met is on a search to discover who she is. In thirty years of counseling, I believe that search has never been harder. There's so much noise—around you and often inside you—that it's hard to find your voice and hear God's voice. I'm so grateful for my friend Kari and this book that speaks directly to the heart of girls. You are deeply loved, delighted in, and far more valuable to God and the world than you can imagine!"

Sissy Goff, LPC/MHSP, therapist, podcast host, and bestselling author of
The Worry-Free Parent

"Kari knows how to counsel, support, encourage, and love young women, and it shows in the pages of this devotional. This book anticipates so many of the situations and struggles that young women experience and face, and it meets those challenges with biblical truth and godly wisdom. I am grateful for this excellent resource."

Cameron Cole, founding chairman of Rooted Ministries: Advancing Gospel-Centered
Youth and Family Ministry, author of *Gospel-Centered Youth Ministry: A Practical Guide*

"Kari has a unique ability to compassionately address the challenges that many young women face, and *Yours, Not Hers* beautifully explores the issues surrounding comparison with a level of understanding that will make readers sigh with relief. More than anything, *Yours, Not Hers* is a forty-day reminder for all of us to look up when we're tempted to look around. Well done, my friend!"

Sophie Hudson, author of *A Fine Sight to See: Leading Because You Were Made for It*
and cohost of *The Big Boo Cast*

"Few voices speak directly into the hearts and minds of teenage girls like Kari Kampakis. She has an incredible way of normalizing their feelings without judgement while offering relatable wisdom to navigate the unique challenges they face today. This devotional is spiritual and psychological gold. In the words of my thirteen-year-old daughter, 'Wow. This is spot on.'"

Niro Feliciano, psychotherapist, author of *This Book Won't Make You Happy* **and** *TODAY*
Show **contributor and columnist**

"Kari has done it again, sharing wisdom and truth while making young women feel seen and known as she relates to their experiences and points them to Scripture. This book is a must-read for all young women."

Grace Valentine, bestselling author, @thegracevalentine

"As a mom of two teens, I buy everything Kari Kampakis writes. She always offers the most beautiful combination of relatable, biblical, and practical thoughts for girls. *Yours, Not Hers* is a must-read for teen girls."

Courtney DeFeo, author of *In This House, We Will Giggle* **and the** *Treasured* **faith-based**
study and host of *Pardon the Mess* **podcast**

Yours, Not Hers

40 DEVOTIONS TO STOP COMPARISONS AND LOVE YOUR LIFE

KARI KAMPAKIS

An Imprint of Thomas Nelson

Yours, Not Hers

Copyright © 2025 Kari Kampakis

Tommy Nelson, PO Box 141000, Nashville, TN 37214

Published in Nashville, Tennessee, by Tommy Nelson. Tommy Nelson is an imprint of Thomas Nelson. Thomas Nelson is a registered trademark of HarperCollins Christian Publishing, Inc.

Published in association with the literary agency of Wolgemuth & Wilson.

Tommy Nelson titles may be purchased in bulk for educational, business, fundraising, or sales promotional use. For information, please email SpecialMarkets@ThomasNelson.com.

ISBN 978-1-4002-4918-3 (audiobook)
ISBN 978-1-4002-4922-0 (eBook)
ISBN 978-1-4002-4921-3 (HC)

Library of Congress Cataloging-in-Publication Data

Names: Kampakis, Kari, 1972- author. Title: Yours, not hers : 40 devotions to stop comparisons and love your life / Kari Kampakis.
Description: Nashville, Tennessee : Thomas Nelson, [2024] | Includes bibliographical references. | Audience: Ages 13+ | Summary: "Discover the guide to true confidence for today's teen and college-age girl! Author and speaker Kari Kampakis helps you stop playing the comparison game and embrace the unique purpose God has for your life. From navigating social media to making friends to deepening your faith, this 40-day devotional will help you become more authentically you"-- Provided by publisher.
Identifiers: LCCN 2024030012 (print) | LCCN 2024030013 (ebook) | ISBN 9781400249213 (hardcover) | ISBN 9781400249220 (epub) Subjects: LCSH: Self-confidence--Relgious aspects--Christianity. | Teenage girls--Religious life.
Classification: LCC BV4598.23 .K43 2024 (print) | LCC BV4598.23 (ebook) | DDC 248.8/33--dc23/eng/20240711 LC record available at https://lccn.loc.gov/2024030012 LC ebook record available at https://lccn.loc.gov/2024030013

Written by Kari Kampakis

Printed in Canada

25 26 27 28 29   TC   6 5 4 3 2

Mfr: TC / Quebec, Canada / January 2025 / PO #12306786

To Alexis Dermatas, my angel

━━━━━━━━━━

The grace of God means something like: "Here is your life. You might never have been, but you are, because the party wouldn't have been complete without you. Here is the world. Beautiful and terrible things will happen. Don't be afraid. I am with you. Nothing can ever separate us. It's for you I created the universe. I love you."

Frederick Buechner[1]

Contents

CONTENTS

A Note from the Author

Chances are, you feel confident some days. You feel brave and bold, ready to take on the world.

But then you look around. You notice the girls beside you, and suddenly your confidence shrinks. Social media makes it worse as it allows your comparisons to expand to every girl on the planet.

Rather than embrace *your* life, you suddenly wish you had *her* life. You start to worry that you don't measure up in one or more areas of life:

- » Friendships
- » Popularity
- » Beauty
- » Academics
- » Achievements
- » Dating
- » Finances
- » Fashion
- » Happiness

The comparison game is exhausting, isn't it? And ultimately, it will crush your soul. It isn't just a game when it disrupts your life purpose and leaves you starved for real connection.

Thankfully, there is freedom—freedom that begins with God. He made you on purpose for this moment in time. He created you to serve your generation like no one has ever served before.

By embracing God's unique plan for you and running the race that *you* were born to run, you can unlock your full potential without sneaking sideways glances at the girls running beside you. You can champion them as they run their races too.

I have a big heart for teenage girls because I'm raising four girls myself. I remember being your age and all the inner wrestling I did as I struggled with perfectionism, anxiety, self-doubt, body image, and never feeling good enough.

Today, as a writer and speaker, I meet thousands of teenage girls and their moms. They share their deepest struggles, and as I listen to the challenges your generation is facing, I realize this:

The world that is shaping you is harder, darker, and meaner than the world that shaped previous generations. You need to be stronger and smarter than we were at your age—and more rooted in what is real.

In this broken world, you *will* face troubles (John 16:33). You'll have crosses to bear, mountains to climb, and fears to conquer.

But by anchoring your life to the hope of Jesus, you'll be

able to weather the storms. You'll make it through your trials, crises, and life-altering events. You won't have to live in fear because He promises to never leave you (Hebrews 13:5). The One who lives in you is greater than the Enemy who lives in the world (1 John 4:4).

This devotional is designed to inspire the best version of you. Even if you're shy or reserved by nature, you can be brave and bold for Jesus. You may not be perfect, but you *are* remarkable, and you have a significant role to play in God's master plan.

So don't let the world miss out on knowing the real you. Don't shrink back, downplay your gifts, or believe the lie that your life doesn't matter. Instead, stay focused on how Jesus sees you. Avoid the distraction and discouragement that always come when you play the comparison game.

Your life is God's gift to you, and what you do with your life is your gift back to God. Join me in this forty-day journey to discover what sets you apart and celebrate those truths that set you free.

Cheering for you,
Kari Kampakis

DAY 1

Love

I am convinced that nothing can ever separate us from God's love. Neither death nor life, neither angels nor demons, neither our fears for today nor our worries about tomorrow—not even the powers of hell can separate us from God's love.

Romans 8:38

A sixteen-year-old girl told me about an expensive dress that she wore *once* in eighth grade, and she refuses to wear it again.

Why? Because when she looks back, she doesn't like her eighth-grade self. She wishes that she'd been a kinder person.

1

And when she sees that dress, those memories come flooding back.

Believe it or not, her self-reflection is an act of courage—and proof of her maturity. It shows how God has worked in her heart to help her grow up and evolve.

Many people, even adults, are too prideful to admit their past mistakes. They don't want to examine their past or can't handle being wrong because it challenges their need to believe that they are a good and decent person.

Rather than go to that uncomfortable place, they bury unpleasant thoughts or point fingers at other people to deflect attention off themselves. This may look like a girl who removes friends from group texts and denies that this is mean behavior. Or a boy who blames his girlfriend for making him cheat because she set physical boundaries with him.

Seeing the truth about ourselves—with all our flaws, blind spots, and failures—can be difficult. It can lead to self-hatred or shame.

Our world expects perfection, and since we're prone to chase that standard, it's a major blow to the ego to fall short of that ideal. It can make us believe destructive lies, like thinking we're too inadequate, too broken, or too far gone to deserve love or a remarkable life.

Yet here is the crazy truth: Even on your worst days, God loves you. Even in your rock-bottom moments, He sees your beauty and potential.

God loves you even when you aren't kind to others. Even when you bomb a test. Even when you feel angry at Him and are tempted to walk away. He doesn't love you because you are good—He loves you because *He* is good, and nothing you do can change that.

What God creates, God loves, and what God loves, He loves forever.

We have all sinned and fallen short of God's glory. We are all sinners in need of a Savior. Scripture says this, yet it also tells us how there is no condemnation for those who belong to Jesus. Anyone who belongs to Him becomes a new creation, for the old life is gone, and a new life has begun (Romans 3:23; Romans 8:1; 2 Corinthians 5:17).

Thankfully, this means that you are made new through Jesus. God's mercies are new each morning. Who you're becoming today matters more than who you've been in the past, and you're not chained to or imprisoned by your past mistakes or your eighth-grade self. Even your most embarrassing moments or that ridiculous thing you once did can be left in the past as you move forward with Jesus.

Nothing can separate you from His love *except* your refusal to accept it.

God's love is a game changer that transforms your life. It helps you see yourself through His eyes and not feel ashamed of your humanity. Even self-reflection takes a comforting turn when you feel so secure in God's love that you can lay your ugliest truths on the table to begin your transformation.

You can be honest, humble, and curious—and trust that God can use it all for His glory and your good.

Take time today to reflect on God's love for you. Find peace in knowing that through every phase and season of change, God's love for you is constant. You just have to accept it.

*Lord, show me what You see. Help me believe
that I'm deeply loved so I can love myself
and others. Thank You for Your patience
when I fall short. Thank You for believing
in me when I lose faith in myself. Amen.*

Reflection Questions

1. Do you live like a girl who knows she is loved or like a girl who tries to prove her worth? Share where you are right now.

2. Feeling confident in who you are helps you to be honest about yourself with others, even as you admit hard truths. In 2 Corinthians 12:9, Paul said he could *boast* about his weaknesses since God's power is made perfect in weakness. Are you confident enough in God's love to boast about your weaknesses, or would you like to grow in this area?

3. Do you believe that God forgives your sins when you confess them with a heart that's truly sorry? Do you keep replaying the past and refuse to forgive yourself? Explain.

_____

_____

_____

_____

_____

_____

_____

A FINAL THOUGHT

It's hard to love yourself when you aren't proud of things you've done. And when you struggle to love yourself, you'll struggle to love others too. Thankfully, Jesus can help. He offers you a *new way*, a *new life*, and a *new heart*. Rather than feel stuck with the worst choice you ever made (or your biggest regret), you can enjoy freedom through Him. You can turn a new leaf or get a fresh start. Ask God to heal you through His transformative love. Pray for faith to believe you're worthy and for humility to recognize this undeserved blessing.

Loneliness

Draw near to God, and he
will draw near to you.

James 4:8 ESV

A freshman girl at a large university pledged a sorority, but she didn't know anyone since she was from out of state.

All around her, she watched her pledge sisters connect. Since many of them had grown up together or knew one another previously, the friend groups and alliances formed quickly.

This situation can cause many girls to fall into panic mode. They mentally spiral and imagine their future as one big social defeat. They may act clingy as they desperately try to make new friends. Or they may retreat to their dorm room and binge-watch Netflix as they wait to be invited.

But that's not what this college freshman did. Instead, she put herself in social situations. She attended Bible studies, church, and activities, even though it meant going alone. Since lunchtime at her sorority house attracted a flood of girls, she sat on the couch every day during this time to meet people. She knew this would improve her odds of finding friends she clicked with.

And that's exactly what happened. She eventually found her people *and* found her place within the sorority because she was willing to be brave. She refused to let loneliness have the final say.

We all feel lonely at times because we're all on unique paths. While our paths may intersect, allowing us to journey together, we also face seasons when we walk alone. Everyone experiences loneliness, and before high school even ends, you're likely to feel lonely in situations like these:

- » Being left out of a gathering or a big event
- » Watching your friends (or friendships) change
- » Facing the consequences of a mistake
- » Getting ghosted or cut out of a group
- » Losing someone you love
- » Being away from home
- » Feeling unwanted or invisible
- » Walking through a personal trial

Loneliness can hit us unexpectedly, but we all experience it at times.

In these seasons, lean into your faith. Let the insecurity

you feel deepen your dependence on God. Even when you feel alone, He is present, always walking before you and beside you. He understands your deepest sorrows and collects your tears in a bottle (Deuteronomy 31:8; Psalm 56:8).

When you feel lonely, don't struggle alone. Don't believe the dangerous lie that no one cares about you or wants you around.

Asking for help doesn't show weakness—it shows that you're smart. It means you're staying ahead of your pain or your problem. Since God created you for community, He places people on your path when you need them. When you share your lonely struggle with someone you trust (a parent, friend, or counselor), you open the door for God to speak.

You give that person a chance to share *their* lonely story with you. Everyone has one, I promise.

I can recall one very lonely night in high school when a friend who took me to prom (who I didn't treat well) told me that his friends didn't like me after the way I handled that date. I loved his friends, so this was hard to hear, and I wondered if everyone hated me. I felt alone in my mistake.

But God never wastes pain, and even when your loneliness is self-induced like mine was that night, He is still hard at work. He's stretching you, softening you, and comforting you. He's building your self-awareness and strength.

God can help you dig deep for courage. He equips you to admit your struggles, make things right, and bravely connect with others.

All around you, every day, there are other girls who feel lonely too. They're waiting for someone to notice—for someone like you to take that first step and initiate a potential new friendship.

8

*Lord, give me the resolve to be proactive.
Help me push through awkward feelings
and anxieties to find my community. Show
me who to trust and what friends I should
seek. Comfort me when I feel lonely so I can
comfort others who feel lonely too. Amen.*

Reflection Questions

1. When loneliness hits you, how do you respond? Do you with-draw, or do you find someone to process your feelings with?

_____

_____

_____

_____

_____

2. Are you outgoing by nature, or do you need a pep talk to leave home? What brave steps can you take to put yourself in more social situations?

_____

_____

_____

_____

3. What have lonely seasons taught you? How have they made you more attuned to others who feel lonely?

_____

_____

_____

_____

_____

_____

_____

_____

A FINAL THOUGHT

You are fearfully and wonderfully made (Psalm 139:14). You are *not* a mistake or a nuisance. It's easy to doubt yourself or believe your loneliness will last forever when you feel overlooked, excluded, or cast aside, but it won't. There are moments of joy ahead (including connecting with other people!) that God has planned for you. So let your lonely seasons make you a more compassionate, welcoming, and intuitive friend. Let those times be the catalyst that leads to real community.

Purpose

For we are God's handiwork, created in
Christ Jesus to do good works, which
God prepared in advance for us to do.

Ephesians 2:10 NIV

D o you ever feel like you're drifting through life, waiting for something spectacular to happen? And day after day, when nothing out of the ordinary occurs, do you wonder if your life matters?

At some point, we all question our purpose. We wonder if we're special or just another face in the crowd. From this place of doubt, our minds can spiral. They can take us to a hopeless place where we discount our value.

11

But please remember this: **your life *does* matter, and any dark thoughts you have are *not* from God.** He created you to live with a spirit of strength, not defeat. And your greatest life purpose—greater than any spectacular moment—is to know, love, and serve Him. As you embrace this purpose, you create a life of meaning.

You become part of God's great rescue mission to save humankind.

The question is, How do you discover what God has prepared for you? What clues point toward your purpose? Consider these questions:

» What hobby or activity makes you lose track of time?
» What skill or talent comes more easily to you than the average person?
» What work would you do for free because you love it so much?
» What makes you feel like a girl on a mission?
» What makes you feel happy, energized, and in your zone?
» What do you have a sharp memory for? Is it stories, names, sports, relationships, home décor, health, finance, languages, gardening, history, or something else?
» What has sparked a sense of purpose in you? Was it helping your mom with Thanksgiving dinner, playing with little kids, serving at a shelter, or hearing your English teacher praise your essay? (Little moments of joy can offer big clues about your best place of impact.)

Philippians 2:13 says, "For God is working in you, giving you the desire and the power to do what pleases him."

The stirrings in your heart aren't random or accidental; God planted them there. They are meant to draw you into His will.

This is why you may be fascinated with sign language while your friend likes journalism. Maybe you love to bake while your sister prefers to sew. It's the same God distributing unique gifts to bring light into our broken world.

Please hear me when I say this: Now, more than ever, we need your light. People are starving for hope and goodness, and through your sphere of influence, you have abundant opportunities to turn someone's day around.

Drawing even *one* heart closer to God or helping *one* person get to heaven is a level of success far greater than your most spectacular moments. Showing God's love in tangible ways can change someone's life trajectory and inspire purpose in their life.

Your talents are designed to point people to God, not to point people to you. Don't waste your gifts or assume they aren't relevant because our world needs you. Your presence here *matters*. You have a purpose to fulfill.

So, rather than drift through life, live like a girl on a mission. Use your gifts to make an eternal difference in the lives of people you know.

---

*Lord, show me my purpose. Reveal what I
was born to do, and empower me to do it.
When self-doubt talks, let Your voice be louder.
Use me to point people to You. Amen.*

Reflection Questions

1. Name a time when you felt *needed*—when someone needed your help, and your presence, idea, or talent made a positive difference. How do these moments point you toward purpose? Why do you feel uplifted afterward?

_____

_____

_____

_____

_____

_____

2. In God's kingdom, there is power found in *one*. Helping *one* person find their way means more than ten thousand "likes" on Instagram. Describe ways to use your talent to make an eternal difference in someone's life.

_____

_____

_____

_____

_____

_____

_____

3. Purpose comes from serving the person in front of you. Whether someone needs a friend, an invitation, or an encouraging word, it is all an opportunity to honor God. How can you better notice these needs moving forward?

_____

_____

_____

_____

_____

_____

_____

A FINAL THOUGHT

Imagine taking a class and refusing to listen to the teacher. She gives you all the tools you need to succeed, but you tune her out. You do it your way, and you fail. This is what happens when you do life without God. He knows you because He made you. He created you for a purpose that only you can serve. Work with Him and know that every morning when you wake up with a pulse, you also wake up with a purpose. God has assignments prepared for you that only you can carry out.

Beauty

The LORD said to Samuel, "Do not consider his appearance or his height, for I have rejected him. The LORD does not look at the things people look at. People look at the outward appearance, but the LORD looks at the heart."

1 Samuel 16:7 NIV

P retty is as pretty does." For many years this timeless truth has been passed down by mothers, grandmothers, and life mentors.

What they know—and want you to know—is that a girl's behavior impacts her beauty. Many outwardly beautiful girls make themselves ugly by acting catty, manipulative, selfish, or arrogant.

Nothing destroys a pretty face faster than a mean personality or a lack of integrity.

If you haven't witnessed this already, you will. It may be a girl who you envy and look up to because she is drop-dead gorgeous. You may find yourself staring at her, taking mental notes, and maybe copying an outfit or two.

But then one day, her character is revealed. Your opinion suddenly changes as you see her trash-talk a friend, make fun of someone, or turn into a bully.

It doesn't take long to figure out that beauty gives a girl power. It attracts attention, opens doors, and makes people take notice. Some girls abuse this power by hurting others to help themselves get ahead. Despite the effort they put in as they get ready for their day, their beauty routine misses a key ingredient: **They don't have God in their heart. And without God in your heart, you can't possess real beauty.**

Real beauty starts in the heart, and throughout Scripture, God makes it clear that a beautiful heart is more important than a beautiful face. Since your heart is the starting point for your thoughts, actions, and choices, it impacts the direction that you take.

This is why God says in Proverbs 4:23 to guard your heart above all else, for it determines the course of your life.

So, is it wrong to be beautiful? Do all pretty girls abuse their power? Absolutely not. **Our world is full of outwardly beautiful girls who are even more beautiful on the inside.** The better you know them, the prettier they become because God's Spirit makes them radiate.

A girl's heart can be pretty or ugly. It has nothing to do with her physical appearance. The goal, I believe, is to pleasantly surprise people. To let your heart outshine your appearance. To remember that kindness costs you nothing, but being unkind can cost you a lot.

Your heart may be the cornerstone of your beauty, but your physical self matters too because your heart, body, mind, and soul are all interconnected. What is good for one area is good for all areas. Together they strengthen your health and well-being.

So, while you don't want to idolize your appearance, you don't want to neglect it either. After all, how you feel about yourself often impacts your desire to do good. When you care for yourself, you're better able to care for others.

How can you change the world if you're embarrassed to leave home?

How can you thrive if your legitimate human needs are ignored?

As a living creation, you need daily love, care, and nourishment. You are worthy of this time and attention. To neglect yourself is to dismiss the value that God embedded in you.

As you care for yourself, consider where your energy goes. Where do you invest the most time and attention? Do you work as hard to enhance your inner beauty as you do to enhance your outer beauty? Do you realize that as you grow up, your inner beauty will matter even more?

Girls who fail to develop a rich interior life often end up unhappy and empty as their looks begin to fade. Even the star of the show will one day be replaced. Someone younger will become the prettiest girl in the room.

If you believe your beauty only comes from how you look, then it's all downhill from here. The future looks bleak.

But if you see the big picture and understand beauty from the inside out, then your future holds promise. You won't fear getting older and the changes it brings, because the older you get, the more beautiful your heart can become.

You are beautiful because God made you. He designed you in His image with great intention and attention. At every age, you're God's masterpiece, so walk humbly into that truth. Treat others well and see their beauty because they are a masterpiece too.

———————————— ⊣ ⊢ ————————————

Lord, help me prioritize my heart. Make it beautiful and tender. Guard me from petty obsessions that dim Your light inside of me, and create space for that light to grow. Amen.

———————————— ⊣ ⊢ ————————————

Reflection Questions

1. Nobody cheers for you when your heart grows more beautiful. But when your appearance gets a glow-up, the celebration gets loud. How does this outside noise impact what you focus on? What role, if any, does social media play in your pursuit of beauty?

_____

_____

_____

_____

_____

2. Have you ever seen a girl act ugly and realized you've done the same? If so, did you dismiss this epiphany or use it to self-reflect? Explain.

_____

_____

_____

_____

3. How would you explain beauty to a younger girl? What do you wish someone had told you?

_____

_____

_____

_____

A FINAL THOUGHT

Our world is obsessed with outward appearances. The shinier a girl becomes, the more attention and applause she receives. This praise can be intoxicating, but it's also temporary, so put your faith in what lasts. Find a healthy balance in nurturing your heart, body, mind, and soul. Remember that real beauty grows from the inside out. When God's Spirit lives in you, you radiate a beauty that money can't buy.

Self-Image

Thank you for making me so wonderfully
complex! Your workmanship is
marvelous—how well I know it.

Psalm 139:14

When you look in the mirror, what is your reaction? Do you smile at your reflection—or pick yourself apart?

Most of us know that latter category well. When we look at ourselves or think of ourselves, our imperfections jump out first. We focus on what we should "fix."

Your self-image may not feel significant, but for many reasons, it is. Why? Because a lack of confidence keeps you from living fully. Arrogance keeps you from living wisely. Both extremes undermine God's best life for you.

It's understandable if you are hard on yourself because the world can be hard on you. People are quick to judge, criticize, and attack these days. You may be canceled, cast aside, or told that you're worthless.

Even though that's not true—no human gets to decide the worth of another human—it's easy to forget as social media allows unsolicited commentary on your life. It's hard to know who to believe.

Even if you know your worth in your mind, connecting that truth to your heart can be a challenge. After all, you see what people value. You know what draws a crowd. The more perfect a girl appears, and the more charisma she has, the faster her star will rise.

This leads many girls into a "quest to impress" where they begin to

» live for human approval,
» put on a show,
» care more about others' perceptions of them than their perception of themselves, and
» let culture define their self-image.

Sooner or later, this leads to heartache. It puts you at the mercy of fickle human beings prone to change their mind. People can adore you one day and turn on you the next. Their affection isn't guaranteed, and all it takes is one misstep to have a fall from grace.

Why join that emotional roller coaster? **Why put so much faith in the opinions of others when it's impossible to make everyone happy?**

Thankfully, God brings clarity. You have nothing to prove to Him, and you don't need to put on a show to win Him over.

Unlike humans, God is steady. You don't have to be perfect to earn His affection or give Him reasons to like you. Even if others can't see your worth, He is in your corner. He notices when you wander off.

Like the good shepherd who left ninety-nine sheep to search for the one that is missing, God will come for you. And when He finds you, He's happier about that than the ninety-nine sheep that didn't wander (Matthew 18:12–14).

In other words, you're irreplaceable to the Lord.

Remember this as you scrutinize your reflection in the mirror. Never forget that you are lovable, unique, and needed. You don't need to win popularity contests to prove you're something special. Your value comes from God, and peace comes as you learn to think like Him.

Lord, shape my perspective. Show me the way to self-love and self-acceptance. When critiques fill my head, bring the truth to my mind. Help me love myself through Your loving lens. Amen.

23

Reflection Questions

1. Describe yourself in one sentence. Do you think God would agree or disagree with your assessment?

_____

_____

_____

_____

_____

_____

2. Name a past event (a hurtful remark, a life-changing night, a major rejection) that distorted your self-image. How did it make you doubt yourself, lose yourself, or shrink back?

_____

_____

_____

_____

_____

_____

_____

3. Have you ever embarked on a "quest to impress"? If so, what happened?

_____

_____

_____

_____

_____

_____

_____

_____

_____

_____

A FINAL THOUGHT

One common mistake that girls make when forming their self-image is going to extremes. You can think too *little* of yourself or too *much* of yourself. You can assume the world would be better without you or assume the world exists for you. A healthy self-image is found in the middle. It starts by seeing yourself as a child of God and believing He made you for a great purpose.

Friends

There are "friends" who destroy each other,
but a real friend sticks closer than a brother.

Proverbs 18:24

My friend's teenage son got in trouble at school and was sent to the principal's office.

In an uncharacteristic move for him, he had insulted another boy in the hall. His parents were heartbroken and disappointed, and when he got home, they asked him about his actions. What compelled him to do this?

Their son answered honestly. "You wouldn't believe how many guys in my class started to be nice to me after I said that!"

This story is just one example of why your friend choices matter. No matter what choices you make or what lifestyle you choose, you can always find friends who cheer you on and make you *feel* like you're on the right track.

But you can get cheered on by the wrong people. With bad company by your side, you can be on the fast track to self-destruction and not see the warning signs as your friends laugh and egg you on.

Good friends help you become the best version of yourself. They bring you closer to the people who love you most, like your family and oldest friends.

Bad friends, on the other hand, create division in your life. The influence they have in your life may lead you to fight more with your mom, lie to your dad, and act meaner toward your siblings.

"Bad company corrupts good character" (1 Corinthians 15:33), and the trouble with trouble is that it always starts off fun. It seems harmless at first, especially since bad influences tend to be charming.

But you are fooling yourself if you think you can spend time with bad friends and not have them rub off on you. As the old saying goes, "If you hang around the barbershop long enough, you're going to get a haircut." Sooner or later, you'll do what your friends are doing.

So choose friends who you admire and want to emulate, not friends who test the limits and get you sent to the principal's office.

Many girls struggle to set healthy boundaries with bad influences after being taught to "love everyone." They don't understand how to kindly distance themselves from people who stir up trouble or repeatedly hurt them.

Please remember: There are different levels of love. Some

people you can love up close and personal because they're trustworthy and good for you. You can let your guard down and share your heart. They care about you and your future. They've proven to be real friends.

Other people you love at an arm's distance. You are kind and you wish them well, but you set healthy boundaries. You don't answer their probing questions or share your secrets because they may use them against you. Instead, you engage in small talk. You chat about your favorite sports team, homecoming, and superficial topics. You pray for their heart to change, but until that happens, healthy boundaries are needed.

You can love everyone and still carefully choose your innermost circle. There is wisdom in being selective about who you trust most. Trust isn't earned over a weekend, a spring break trip, or your first semester of college. It takes time to observe a friend's choices, see their true colors, and build a shared history.

And if you realize that your friend is a bad influence, you don't have to publicly denounce them or tell them you're cutting ties. You don't have to blatantly say, "You're toxic, and we can't hang out!"

Instead, quietly pull back and invest in other friendships. Spend less time together. Don't badmouth your friend, burn bridges, or underestimate what God can do. You never know who may turn a new leaf or have a major plot twist in their life story.

Relationships happen for a reason, a season, or a lifetime. Even bad friends can serve a purpose by teaching you what you don't want in a friend. Most people can count their best friends on one hand, and if you have this, you're lucky. Just as you would rather have four quarters than a hundred pennies, it's better to have a few real friends than many acquaintances.

Good friends will bring you joy, not unexpected trouble. They'll inspire you to love God more. Find friends who bring out your best, and return the favor to them.

———————————————— ⊢ ⊢ ————————————————

Lord, thank You for the gift of friendship.
Thank You for the perfect friend I always have
in Jesus. Help me set healthy expectations
and give grace when needed. Protect me from
friends who distract me from You. Amen.

———————————————— ⊢ ⊢ ————————————————

Reflection Questions

1. Someone once said, "Show me your friends, and I'll show you your future." Do you believe this? How have your friends shaped your future?

_____

_____

_____

_____

2. Name three red flags of unhealthy friendships. When have you noticed these in your own relationships?

_____

_____

_____

3. Have you ever acted mean to make people like you? If so, did you regret it? Did you apologize, or is that an apology you still owe?

_____

_____

_____

_____

_____

_____

_____

_____

A FINAL THOUGHT

The secret to friendship is to be a great friend first. It's been said that "water seeks its own level," and this means you attract friends like you. If you're kind, you'll attract kind friends. If you're negative, you'll attract negative friends. Your vibe attracts your tribe. Many girls search for good friends, yet few girls make that same effort to *be* a good friend. Real relationships start when two people have God in their hearts and feel drawn to that light in each other.

Boys

Whoever walks with the wise becomes wise,
but the companion of fools will suffer harm.

Proverbs 13:20 ESV

The best way to approach boys is as potential friends, not potential boyfriends.

Why? Because this keeps you real. It inspires the genuine you. If a boy doesn't like the genuine you, that simply means you aren't compatible. This is helpful to know up front.

Girls often see boys as prizes to be won rather than friends to be made. They feel the need to impress them.

But the harder you try to impress a boy, the less you act like yourself. This can make you come across as fake, and who

31

likes an imposter? Who enjoys the company of someone who puts up a front?

Consider the reverse. Imagine discovering that a guy you like hasn't been real with you. What if you'd only seen his sweet, charming, attentive side—and then you discovered that when you weren't present, he acted dismissive and rude? That he doesn't really love snow skiing, hiking, and dogs; he just said that to impress you. Wouldn't that raise red flags? Wouldn't he lose your trust?

Relationships thrive on honesty, and when you aren't honest, a healthy relationship is impossible. You will date (and marry) to your level of health. And the way to attract honest guys is to be an honest girl.

Choosing which boys to allow in your life is much like choosing friends. Be wise and listen to the people who love you, because nothing will get you sidetracked faster than a misguided romance.

A good guy will bring out your best. Even if you break up, you won't regret the relationship because he helped you grow in positive ways.

I know moms who tell their sons, "When you bring a girl home from a date, she should be in better condition than when you picked her up." They teach their boys to *enrich* a girl's life. They want their sons to be protectors, not predators, and to bring out the best in girls, just as girls should do for boys.

In a world that has lost its moral code and where pornography has warped ideas of romance and dating, many boys view girls as merely sexual conquests. Rather than see a sister in Christ, they see an opportunity. Rather than see a person, they see an object. Even a sweet-talking boyfriend can fool you.

One sophomore girl thought her boyfriend hung the

moon until his baseball team urged her to break up with him. Apparently, her boyfriend kept bragging to the team about the lewd actions he planned to take on her, and they got mad. This girl was their friend, and they protected her from forces she couldn't see.

You benefit tremendously from having good guy friends like this. A good guy will tell you what a boy is *really* like. He will go after any jerk who preys on you and will protect you from things that you can't see.

Even if you hope for a boyfriend and want to get married one day, building strong friendships now sets the stage for that future. The world is full of love stories that began as friendships, and the teenage years offer many opportunities to learn about friendship with the opposite sex.

After all, a romance needs chemistry *and* friendship to thrive. Many girls skip the friendship part and dive straight into passion, but passion without friendship won't last. It makes you easy to replace. Friendship is the glue that holds a couple together when times get tough or when the fireworks fade.

The best guys also make fantastic friends. They offer a refreshing reprieve from girl drama and make you laugh and feel good about yourself. If a romance is meant to be, it will happen in God's timing. It will happen because you felt comfortable enough to let a boy see the real you.

Lord, show me the boys I need in my life.
Give me strong instincts, good judgment,
and wisdom to know who to spend time
with. Keep Your hand on my future husband
if marriage is part of my plan. Amen.

Reflection Questions

1. Are you comfortable talking to boys? Explain how your family dynamics (all brothers, all sisters, or whatever your family makeup is) may play a role.

_____

_____

_____

_____

_____

_____

2. What guys in your life do you most enjoy spending time with? Is it your father, grandfather, brother, cousin, or best friend? What makes their perspective different, helpful, or interesting?

_____

_____

_____

_____

_____

_____

3. Have you ever been fooled by a boy you thought you could trust? If so, what did you learn?

_____

_____

_____

_____

_____

_____

_____

_____

_____

A FINAL THOUGHT

Our culture will encourage you to use your beauty, charm, and sex appeal to manipulate boys. It will tell you to toy with their emotions, cry to get what you want, dress provocatively, demand excess attention, and flirt to boost your ego. This isn't a path God blesses, and it ultimately leads to heartache, dysfunction, resentment, and feeling used. Treat boys like friends, and you'll attract the guys worth knowing, the ones with the most potential to be fantastic husbands and fathers one day.

Idols

"I am the Lord your God, who rescued
you from the land of Egypt, the
place of your slavery. You must not
have any other god but me."

Exodus 20:2–3

When it comes to idols, you may assume you don't have any. After all, you're not like the ancient Greeks, who built shrines to false gods and goddesses. Clearly, *they* had an idolatry problem.

But the truth is, we all have idols that we worship in the secret shrines of our hearts. God created us to worship Him, and if He's not our number one, it means we've found a substitute. We've elevated something in His place. We've taken a *good* thing in our life and made it our *ultimate* thing.

Here are some common idols we worship:

» Friends
» Boys
» Beauty
» Fashion
» Popularity
» Celebrities
» Fame
» Achievements
» Big dreams and goals

Even perfectionism can be an idol when we obsess over ourselves. As a teenager, I was guilty of this. I thought about myself *a lot*.

This is a common trap for teenagers, and even researchers call adolescence "the narcissistic years" because of this self-focus.[1] It doesn't help that social media makes us all more self-absorbed. We may spend hours thinking about how other people see, treat, and perceive us, yet we don't spend five minutes considering how we see, treat, and perceive *others*.

This is why so many people feel lonely, invisible, and forgotten. When we're busy running around inside our own heads, we forget to notice others.

Real love considers the needs of the people around us—it is selfless, or "less of self." Relationships work best when both people are selfless. But in egocentric times like these, we're told to "look out for number one." We adopt mentalities such as, "If it's good for me, who cares what it means for someone else?" and then wonder why our relationships feel shallow.

Another common trap during adolescence is to slip into idol worship with someone you love. You may unknowingly put your boyfriend, friend, or favorite celebrity on a pedestal.

But as one priest told my friend after a difficult college breakup: *men make terrible gods.* Friends make terrible gods too, and so do celebrities who seem superhuman but are just as flawed as you and me.

Because in time, anyone on a pedestal will disappoint you, upset you, or let you down. They'll fail to live up to impossible expectations. People should be *part* of your universe but never the *center* of your universe. No human is meant to be your be-all and end-all.

Thankfully, God saves you from yourself. He gives the first and greatest commandment to help you resist the lure of false idols: love the Lord your God with all your heart, mind, and soul (Matthew 22:37).

When God is on your pedestal, nothing else has room to be your number one. **This sets the stage for healthy relationships based on selfless love, not idol worship.**

It takes courage to name your idols and self-awareness to identify what holds you back. Keep your priorities straight by committing first to God.

Lord, show me the idols in my life. Point me toward right-ordered living, and help me admit where I need help. Thank You for loving me when I fail to love You. Thank You for saving me from myself. Amen.

Reflection Questions

1. What idol do you prioritize above God? How would you feel if you suddenly lost it?

2. Have you ever felt hurt or disillusioned by someone you put on a pedestal? If so, what did you learn?

3. Has anyone ever put *you* on a pedestal? If so, did you enjoy the adulation, or did the pressure feel uncomfortable?

_____

_____

_____

_____

_____

_____

_____

_____

_____

A FINAL THOUGHT

Your idols will change as you grow up. While your current idols might be your friend group, your image, your GPA, your wardrobe, or something else, your future idols might be your job, your husband, living in the right neighborhood, or raising perfect kids. Learn to identify your idols and what rules your heart. Make a habit of addressing small obsessions so they don't morph into big obsessions.

Body Image

For we know that when this earthly tent we live in is taken down (that is, when we die and leave this earthly body), we will have a house in heaven, an eternal body made for us by God himself and not by human hands.

2 Corinthians 5:1

I remember the incident clearly: my babysitter declared how heavy I was as she tried to lift me into a cheer stunt.

I was nine years old, shy, and overweight. I didn't want to be lifted, but she insisted. Then she embarrassed me in front of my sisters as she struggled to raise me from under the arms and loudly noted that I was heavier than her friend—*who was seven years older than me!*

I know this babysitter wasn't trying to be mean. She just made a careless remark. And though she probably doesn't remember it, her words left a scar on me and made me hate my body for years to come.

Chances are, you've also heard a remark or two that shaped the way you look at your body. For better or for worse, those remarks set the stage for what you see when you look in the mirror.

Maybe someone commented on your ears, your ankles, or your knobby knees. Maybe they criticized your thighs or the way your bottom looked in certain jeans. Maybe they said you were "too skinny" and told you to eat a burger. Maybe they teased you about your freckles or your childbearing hips.

People take great liberty in scrutinizing the bodies of others. They comment freely and fail to consider the scars they leave.

Social media can make you feel even worse as you are inundated with images of filtered (and seemingly flawless) bodies. Rather than embrace the features you have, you may feel inadequate, jealous, or more discontent with your body.

It only takes one distraction, right? One image that discourages you. One comment that messes with your mind and shapes your body narrative.

The good news is, God wants to help you. He doesn't want you to waste your time obsessing over unrealistic standards.

Does God care about your health? Yes, He does. He gave you your body as a gift, and it's your job to be a good steward of that gift. To fuel your body by drinking water and eating nourishing food, then moving your body to improve your health.

You only get one body, and it has to last you your entire life, so caring for your body today sets you up for a healthy tomorrow. It improves your quality of life.

But God never intended for your body to be a self-improvement project. He doesn't want you to be at war with the body that hosts your beautiful soul.

You see, your body is a temple. It's where God lives in you through the Holy Spirit. He wants you to honor Him with it (1 Corinthians 6:19–20). Rather than fixate on your body's visual appeal, celebrate what it can do. See it as an instrument to share His love.

Does your friend need a hug? *Use your arms to embrace her.*

Is your grandmother lonely? *Use your legs to visit her.*

Is your little sister frustrated with math? *Use your mind to help her.*

Does your mom need to smile? *Use your hands to play the piano that lightens her mood.*

Through your body, you make an invisible God feel real. You build up the body of Christ, a divine community of believers. You bring hope, healing, and joy.

Regardless of what anyone says, your body is holy and good. It deserves love, not punishment, and to be treated like a friend.

Even if you're still working on areas that you neglected in the past, you can love your body. God loves you in every condition. His love doesn't fluctuate even if your jean size does.

One day, when your earthly life ends, your body will no longer matter. At your funeral, people won't be talking about your sculpted abs, your tiny waist, or your thigh gap. What they will talk about is the kind of person you were and how you touched their lives.

The way your body looks won't make you a better person. But the way you use your body while you're here on earth can help you bless others. Your body can be your partner in creating a legacy you feel proud of.

So let that be the thought you wrap your mind around. Let that shape the narrative you believe about the one body you've been given.

———————————————┤ ├———————————————

Lord, help me love the skin I'm in. Show me how to care for my body with lifelong health in mind. Use me to show love through words, actions, laughter, and hugs. Surround me with people who do the same. Amen.

———————————————┤ ├———————————————

Reflection Questions

1. On a scale of one to ten, how do you feel about your body? What recurring thought has been a source of dissatisfaction?

_____

_____

_____

_____

_____

2. What inspires you to take care of your body? Do you simply hope to rock a bikini? Or do you want to feel better, think better, sleep better, live better, and love better? How can this mindset keep you from idolizing fitness and health?

_____

_____

3. What body narrative do you tell yourself? What truth can
   replace the lies you believe?

A FINAL THOUGHT

Many girls (and women) struggle with body image issues. It's a tale as old as time. But when you fixate on how your body looks, you forget what your body can do. You fail to see your bigger purpose of becoming the hands and feet of Jesus. Take care of yourself and be attentive to your body, but keep your efforts in check. Remember that your current body is a temporary home for a soul that lives forever.

Choices

Do not be deceived: God cannot be
mocked. A man reaps what he sows.
Whoever sows to please their flesh,
from the flesh will reap destruction;
whoever sows to please the Spirit,
from the Spirit will reap eternal life.

Galatians 6:7–8 NIV

My parents said I couldn't go, so I decided to be
sneaky. I spent the night with my friend, who set
up a double date with her boyfriend and his friend
who had a crush on me.

I felt flattered by this attention from a popular high

school senior who had just graduated. I was barely fifteen, and only six months earlier I'd gotten my braces off. This felt like exciting new territory for me!

Our age difference didn't faze me, but it sure bothered my parents, so I went behind their back.

Our double date was fun and included dinner and a movie. But when the guys brought us home, my friend's mother met us at the door. The somber look on her face told us something was wrong.

"Kari," she said, "your parents just called. They want you to come home *now*. They know about the date."

Somehow, I'd gotten busted. And I felt humiliated to my core.

My parents grounded me for several weeks. As a teenager, I was mad at them, but as an adult, I agree with their decision. I would never let my daughter date a boy three grades ahead of her either. At that age, there is a huge difference.

What I didn't realize then is that just because you *can* do something doesn't mean you *should* do something. God gives each of us the gift of free will, but making a poor choice (like sneaking behind your parents' back) will always lead to problems.

It may bring punishment or something worse.

Every choice you make has a consequence. And the choices you make now, on your journey to young adulthood, matter tremendously. They set the stage for your future and life trajectory. They may impact you for a lifetime.

The people who love you most, like your parents, understand this. That's why they care about your choices and the consequences that follow.

Even seemingly small choices, like the friend group you land in, determine your life direction. Girls often end up in places they don't want to be because a friend or boyfriend led them there.

One friend of mine, for instance, liked a cute boy in high school who was sweet to her, but he ran with a wild crowd. She didn't see an issue with this until they went on their first date—and he took her to a drug dealer's house! She now tells her daughters, "Even though I was innocent, I would have been arrested if the cops had come. I was guilty by association just by being there."

On the flip side, I have another friend who *was* a wild child in high school. He and his friends loved to party, yet deep in his heart, he knew that he'd never achieve his life goals without more boundaries and self-discipline.

Since his parents never set rules for him, he found discipline by enrolling at The Citadel, a military college in Charleston. Today he is a successful husband, father, and businessman, yet he realizes how different his path could have been after watching his two best friends from high school become alcoholics.

Making good choices for yourself is an act of self-love. It shows that you value your life, your future, and your God-given gifts.

As humans, we all sin and make poor choices at times, but God's grace is bigger than any mistake. He can rescue you from your rock-bottom moments and transform you through the Holy Spirit.

At the same time, you'll reap what you sow in life. You'll live with the consequences of your unique sins and poor choices. You must ask yourself whether those poor choices are worth it in the end.

If you skip class and don't study, then your grades and opportunities will suffer.

If you live on junk food, then your health will suffer.

If you surround yourself with troublemakers, then you'll end up in trouble too.

If you lie and cheat, then your reputation and credibility will suffer.

It's impossible to live a positive life while making negative choices. **And of all the choices you'll make, the most essential one is your choice to follow Jesus.** With Him, you have the ultimate guide. You have a wise friend who never steers you wrong.

When it comes to your life, you always have a choice. You don't *have* to follow the crowd. You don't *have* to stay at a party that's getting too wild. You're allowed to ditch a date who is being disrespectful or leave a job that feels blatantly wrong.

People will often pressure you to make choices that benefit them, but the path to peace is always paved with making choices that please God.

We are all *one* bad choice away from getting off track. We all need humility and compassion for those who get misguided. When you make a wrong turn, don't follow it up with a second wrong turn. Don't assume you've gone too far to stop and turn around.

Instead, learn from your mistake. Ask God to forgive you and help you make the right pivot.

Free will is a gracious gift, and like any gift from God, you need wisdom to use it well. **Live within the boundaries of wise freedom. Make choices that are good for you and other people too.**

*Lord, strengthen my decision-making. Draw
closer when my choices force me to stand alone.
Use the peace that surpasses all understanding
to lead me and show me what is right. Teach
me to trust my gut and pay attention to signals,
convictions, and warnings from You. Amen.*

Reflection Questions

1. What's the *best* choice you ever made? What's the *worst* choice you ever made? What happened each time?

2. The great evangelist Paul got a rocky start to his career. He went from arresting Christians to spreading the gospel world-wide and writing a large part of the New Testament after God changed his heart. Do you believe God can redeem anyone's past? When has God used a mistake you made to bring about something good?

3. Proverbs 12:15 says that fools think their way is right, but the wise listen to others. When making big choices, do you seek wise counsel? Who influences you most?

A FINAL THOUGHT

Decide today what you will (and won't) do. Define your goals and who you hope to be. If you enter new situations saying, "I don't know my plan, but I'll decide when I get there," then you're more likely to cave to peer pressure. You may ignore your better judgment and end up participating in a bad prank, riding with a drunk driver, getting inebriated, trying a random pill, or entering a situation where you're in over your head. Decide ahead of time how you will handle a crossroads moment, and find friends who share your goals.

Trusting God

Many are the plans in the mind of a man, but
it is the purpose of the LORD that will stand.

Proverbs 19:21 ESV

My daughter had doubts about whether to try out for
cheerleading, and her doubts didn't make sense.
After all, she'd cheered since second grade.
Cheer was her life and her passion. She was a valued member
of her high school team, and the skills came easily—until her
sophomore year.

Right before spring tryouts, she got a mental block. She

couldn't complete the tumbling pass and didn't make the varsity team.

Understandably, she was heartbroken, and so were her teammates. She planned to try out again in September for basketball season, but as spring turned into summer, she lost her motivation. She dreaded the tumbling lessons that were once a normal part of her week.

I was on a senior trip with her sister when she texted me: "Mom, what do you think this verse means? I've been praying about whether to try out for cheer, and when I opened my Bible, I saw this."

She sent a screenshot of Proverbs 3:5–6 (ESV):

> **Trust in the LORD with all your heart, and do not lean on your own understanding. In all your ways acknowledge him, and he will make straight your paths.**

My daughter had always been very decisive, and it surprised me to hear this doubt. Immediately I knew that this decision was between her and God, and while I could offer my opinion, I didn't want to interfere with His plan.

I texted her back: "Maybe you feel doubt for a reason. Maybe God has another plan and is leading you in a new direction. It doesn't make sense because cheer has always been central to your life. Keep praying and discerning His voice. Listen to what God says."

She kept praying, and as September drew closer, her answer grew clearer. She would not try out again. She felt sad as she mourned the loss of her dream to cheer for Friday night football games, but she knew this was the best path for her.

Initially, I worried that she'd regret her decision. I

wondered if her skills would suffer if she later changed her mind. But as her junior year kicked in, we saw many blessings emerge from her choice.

One, she was able to handle a rigorous courseload that led to a college scholarship.

Two, she started a new business designing sweatshirts.

And three, she joined the school pageant staff. Her senior year, she was chosen to direct it and planned an amazing show for nine hundred people.

In hindsight it was clear that God had a new plan for her, but on the night of cheer tryouts, all she felt was pain. It hurt to watch this door close.

Chances are, you've had doors close in your life too. You've had your plans interrupted or completely shut down. You've watched friends move forward and leave you behind. You've felt alone in your grief.

In times like these, it's normal to question God. It's normal to feel devastated, angry, or sad. But if you can get through the initial shock, you'll find that life goes on. You'll discover blessings on the other side.

As you wait for those blessings, you can find comfort in words like these:

> » "Jesus replied, 'You don't understand now what I am doing, but someday you will'" (John 13:7).
> » "God's way is perfect. All the LORD's promises prove true. He is a shield for all who look to him for protection" (Psalm 18:30).
> » "I know the LORD is always with me. I will not be shaken, for he is right beside me" (Psalm 16:8).
> » "They do not fear bad news; they confidently trust the LORD to care for them" (Psalm 112:7).

I'm proud of my daughter for trusting God and tuning into His quiet voice. Cheerleading was a big blessing in her life, but like most blessings, it lasted for just a season. When that chapter ended, a new chapter began.

Heartache may be part of your story, but it's not the end of your story. It won't last forever, so hold your head up high. Know that you have new blessings ahead and new chapters being written.

———————————— ⊢ ⊢ ————————————

Lord, sit with me in my sadness. Bring peace as I wait for answers. Help me trust You as the author of my story and praise You for the blessings to come. Amen.

———————————— ⊢ ⊢ ————————————

Reflection Questions

1. Think of a time when God closed a door in your life. How did you feel that day? How did you feel six months later?

_____

_____

_____

_____

2. Have you ever felt led in a new direction that didn't make sense? If so, what did you learn about trusting God?

_____

_____

---

3. Do you believe God can remove a passion from your heart to redirect you? Have you ever experienced this?

A FINAL THOUGHT

Sometimes in life, your best effort isn't good enough. You follow all the rules and do all the right things and still end up brokenhearted. Whether your pain comes from not making the team, falling short of a goal, facing rejection, or not getting the life you dreamed of, it can feel like a gut punch. You wonder if you'll survive. In these moments, remember that God has a plan for you even when your plan falls apart. You can trust Him in the confusion and uncertainty.

DAY 12

Truth

Jesus answered, "I am the way and
the truth and the life. No one comes
to the Father except through me."

John 14:6 NIV

I once dated a boy who cheated on me with another girl.
I suspected that he had, but when I asked him, he lied.
The truth came out three months later, when someone
confirmed my hunch.

He was remorseful and begged for forgiveness. And
though we kept dating, I never fully trusted him again. I
couldn't get over the deceit.

His dishonesty messed with my mind, and at first, I

blamed myself for being gullible. I wondered what was wrong with me. Was I not good enough? Or pretty enough? Or worth being told the truth?

I also questioned my judgment. I was mad at myself for ignoring my instincts. His story had never added up, yet I believed it because I wanted it to be true. I was insecure and liked having a boyfriend.

Now I see his choice as a reflection of *his* character and not *my* desirability. I realize how God brought good from his lie because it taught me to value the truth. Once you've been duped, you hold honesty in high esteem.

Sadly, our world doesn't have a lot of respect for the truth. Many people twist it and tell lies and half-truths without feeling guilty.

Our culture tells us that truth is relative. It says, "You live by your truth, and I'll live by my truth," as if truth depends on one's outlook. But truth is not subjective. It's not decided by you or me. Truth comes from God because God *is* truth.

We can argue with truth, and we can reject it or disagree with it, but we can't change it, because it is settled. **What was true two thousand years ago when Jesus walked this earth, what the Bible preserves as it tells the grand story of God's love, is still true today. It will remain true throughout eternity.**

God's truth will bring you clarity and peace. It's a North Star you can trust. Your most dependable source for truth isn't your favorite TikTok star, the biggest Christian celebrity, or even your best friend. While godly people can help you navigate life and strengthen your faith, nothing will comfort you, empower you, and enlighten you like spending time with God in Scripture.

Lies don't come from God, because God can't lie. He is a

God of peace and order, not confusion and disorder (Hebrews 6:18; 1 Corinthians 14:33). So when a conversation leaves you unsettled or when you can't shake the feeling that there's more to the story than someone is admitting, pay attention to your instincts. Don't let someone convince you of a story that you know deep down isn't true.

The truth will set you free because its origin is in God (John 8:32). But that doesn't mean hearing the truth will always be easy. Sometimes the truth will upset you, hurt you, or scare you. It may be the opposite of what you hoped to hear. But with Jesus as your strength, you can handle heavy news. You can find the peace that comes through honest living and doing the right thing.

Lord, teach me to value the truth. Surround me with trustworthy people, and keep me honest with them and myself. Amen.

Reflection Questions

1. Name a time when someone lied to you. How did this change the value you place on honesty?

2. What lie do you tell yourself? What truth can replace it?

3. When sharing a truth that may upset someone, do you take the most loving approach? How can you speak the truth in love? Explain.

A FINAL THOUGHT

When the truth isn't clear, be patient. Don't rush into decisions, jump to conclusions, or take immediate action. Instead, pray for the facts to come to light. Take time to gather the insight you need to make an informed decision. Sometimes the truth comes at once, and sometimes it unfolds slowly. Either way, God is present, slowly revealing what is hidden.

People-Pleasing

So whether we are at home or away,
we make it our aim to please him.

2 Corinthians 5:9 ESV

Years ago, I wrote a book about living for God's approval, not human approval. I wrote it for teenage girls, but little did I know, I would need the message myself.

When the book released, a mom of a girl in my daughter's grade started a false narrative about me. She tried to turn some moms against me. And while her efforts soon fizzled, it was a blow to feel scorn from a woman I barely knew.

I realized then that I was a people pleaser. I didn't

necessarily care about being popular or the center of attention, but I did want people to like me. It hurt to learn about this campaign where someone chose me as the target.

Thankfully, I'd just written on this subject. I coached myself using the message God gave me. All the hours I'd spent trying to help teen girls came full circle as I remembered these truths:

» God knows the full story and your heart. Focus on pleasing Him, and He'll take care of you.
» What people say about you is opinion, and what God says about you is fact. The way to know your worth is to focus on the facts.
» What a person uses to harm you, God can use for good. Trust Him as your protector.

I didn't badmouth this mom or go to extra lengths to defend myself. Instead, I focused on my family and my work, prayed to see any wrongs I should right, and let people decide for themselves who to believe.

God in His goodness brought me unexpected love and support, and it made this season easier. The drama passed as drama always does.

For most people, especially girls and women, relationships matter. We care deeply about our relationships—yet problems arise when we care more about what people *say* about us than what God *knows* about us. From there we may come unhinged as we fear the social fallout and panic over the future.

You see, being a people pleaser comes with a cost. It makes us fear the loss of human approval more than a lost connection with God.

This may look like any of the following:

» Compromising your values to not ruffle feathers or upset the wrong people
» Saying what your friends want to hear, even if that means telling white lies
» Blaming others, badmouthing others, or pitting people against each other to get a crowd on your side and prove you are "right"
» Doing anything to win over the VIP crowd
» Pretending to be someone you're not
» Letting the gap widen between who you are and who God has called you to be

Even if you're an expert people pleaser, some people won't like you. That's just a fact. I don't say this to discourage you but to alleviate the pressure of chasing an impossible goal. Only God's approval matters, and if you're pleasing Him, you don't have to fear what people say or think. You can rest in truths like these:

» "Fearing people is a dangerous trap, but trusting the LORD means safety" (Proverbs 29:25).
» "Am I now trying to win the approval of human beings, or of God? Or am I trying to please people? If I were still trying to please people, I would not be a servant of Christ" (Galatians 1:10 NIV).
» "What good will it be for someone to gain the whole world, yet forfeit their soul?" (Matthew 16:26 NIV).
» "When a man's ways please the LORD, he makes even his enemies to be at peace with him" (Proverbs 16:7 NKJV).

You might be thinking, *But I don't want to be lonely. I enjoy feeling liked!* I totally get that.

God wired you for community, and that's why you want to be liked. If you didn't care at all, you'd be content as a lifelong loner.

But like any good thing, this desire can become an obsession. It can make you sacrifice who you are and become chained to public opinion.

Looking up solves this problem. It keeps you focused and firm. You don't have to win popularity contests to live an incredible life. Trust me: when you listen to God and pattern your life after His goodness, you'll attract good people. You'll find the love, affirmation, and encouragement you need to carry out your life purpose.

Lord, help me crave a deep relationship with You. Help me live for my audience of One. Let Your voice be the loudest voice in my head and the voice I care about most. Protect me when I need protection. Amen.

Reflection Questions

1. Do you ever struggle with the "disease to please"? Are you ultrasensitive to criticism and not being liked? Explain.

_____

2. Have you ever lied, held back details, or blamed others to earn human approval? If so, what scared you the most about losing approval?

_____

3. Are you the same person no matter who you talk to? Or do you change like a chameleon to win people over? What situations make you stumble?

_____

_____

_____

_____

_____

_____

A FINAL THOUGHT

Being self-aware and noticing how people respond to you is good. For instance, if you tend to speak bluntly, you may notice the hurt look on someone's face when you make an insensitive remark. This teaches you to be careful with your words. It builds your social intelligence. At the same time, it's easy to overanalyze everyone's reaction to you. It's tempting to reinvent yourself for all the wrong reasons—putting on a fake persona, buying better clothes, finding cooler friends, or acting more social just to gain acceptance. Don't let human approval or disapproval dictate your direction. Keep it simple by living to please God.

Faith

Come close to God, and God
will come close to you.

James 4:8

I remember being excited about going to college—because
for the first time in my life, I could choose to skip church.

At last, I had no one to answer to. I could sleep in on
Sunday mornings without my mom waking me up for Mass.

But then a funny thing happened. Early in my freshman year, I met several new friends who happened to be
Catholic too, and they invited me to church. I didn't want
to go, but since I craved more time with them, I said yes and
joined them.

Looking back, I see God's hand in these encounters. Simply going to church was enough to captivate my heart.

The campus priest at the time, Father Ray, was a prolific speaker. He appealed to all ages with his funny stories, warm personality, folksy approach, and ability to make eye contact with each person in the room. Every sermon felt specifically intended for me as he discussed real-life struggles through the lens of faith.

Going to church was my saving grace. Away from my parents and childhood comforts, I discovered that I didn't need God less; I needed Him *more*.

College brought a roller coaster of highs and lows. One day I'd feel on top of the world from meeting so many people; the next day I'd feel lost in the crowd in this world of many unknowns. Having a church brought a welcome security. It tethered me and pulled me home—physically, emotionally, and spiritually—when I began to drift.

In church I remembered who I was: a deeply loved child of God. In those pews I felt peaceful and calm. This setting became my reprieve from the busyness of college life and the noise of the party scene. This is where I learned to own my faith and go to church because I wanted to go, not because my parents made me.

It's where my faith took on a life of its own as I chose to pursue God.

Leaving home presents a huge opportunity to take your faith to the next level. For the first time, you have the option to choose. You get to make a conscious decision about your spiritual journey.

Everyone's journey is different, and your faith journey may feel uniquely complicated. If you've been hurt in the past by a church, you may feel hesitant or put off. If you've never heard of Jesus, you may think that Christianity sounds kind of weird. If you're mad at God due to a hardship you've faced, you may run the other way. You may feel confused about His character if someone has painted a warped picture of who He is.

Wherever you are in your journey right now, Jesus can meet you there. All you need to begin a relationship is an open heart and a desire to truly know Him.

It's normal for your faith to ebb and flow as your life evolves. You may have seasons of amazing growth followed by seasons that feel barren and dry. Some seasons may feel especially dark, like you can't see three feet in front of you. In the darkness you'll feel desperate for any glimmer of light.

Through it all, God stays close. He sees you, hears you, and pursues your heart. He can handle your hardest questions and your rawest emotions. Nothing you do can push Him away, and if you look for Him with all your heart, you *will* find Him. God rewards those who sincerely seek Him (Jeremiah 29:13; Hebrews 11:6).

So make a conscious decision to make your faith your own. Go to church alone, if you must, and invite a friend when you can. You never know how God may use you to impact the journey of a fellow seeker.

Lord, help my unbelief. Give me the desire and the hunger to pursue You. Encourage me through other believers and point me to churches that teach truth and feel like home. Deepen my faith so I can positively impact others. Amen.

Reflection Questions

1. Describe your faith today. Is it lukewarm, strong, complicated, boring, exciting, fleeting, or in a lull? Where are you now, and where do you hope to be?

_____

_____

_____

_____

_____

_____

2. Jesus said that it's not healthy people who need a doctor, but rather, the sick (Luke 5:31). A healthy church should feel more like a hospital for spiritual healing than a courtroom for judgment. Does church feel this way to you? Why or why not?

_____

_____

_____

_____

_____

_____

3. Whose faith journey do you admire? What spiritual habits do they practice (going to church, reading the Bible, practicing virtues like kindness, spending time with God each day, and so on) that you'd like to adopt?

_____

_____

_____

_____

_____

_____

_____

A FINAL THOUGHT

Faith is a personal choice, and while you certainly need mentors, leaders, and friends who sharpen you spiritually as iron sharpens iron (Proverbs 27:17), you can't borrow their faith and count it as your salvation. As you grow up, you must learn to own your faith. You can't piggyback on your mom's faith, your grandpa's faith, or anyone else's faith. God wants a personal relationship with *you*. He has children, not grandchildren, and when you embrace Him as your heavenly Father, you join a family who will live together in eternity.

Prayer

Don't worry about anything; instead, pray about everything. Tell God what you need, and thank him for all he has done.

Philippians 4:6

How do you pray?" A college girl was asked this question by her mother, and it caught her off guard.

She never imagined that her mom would want her advice. But as a Bible study leader, this college girl had cultivated a strong prayer life, and she felt honored that her mom would set aside her ego to seek guidance from someone younger.

Her mom pushed past the awkwardness of asking for help. She admitted that she didn't have all the answers like many adults pretend to do.

I love this story because 1) it shows the mom's humility, 2) it proves you're never too young to inspire or help other believers, and 3) it's a reminder that even adults struggle with prayer at times.

Your prayer life will be unique because *you* are unique. You have a unique way of thinking, talking, and connecting, and because of this, your conversations with God won't sound exactly like anyone else's.

While seeking wise guidance is always a good idea, remember that God wants a personal relationship with *you*. You don't have to be eloquent or savvy for your prayers to be heard; what matters most is your heart and the humility behind your words.

Even simple phrases like *Help me, Jesus* or *Lord, have mercy on me* are prayers. (They're called breath prayers—prayers short enough to say in one breath.) These prayers demonstrate that you submit to God as the authority of your life.

It's easy to treat God like a magic genie and only pray when you have a problem. It's tempting to believe that if you try to live a perfect life, God will reward your choices and good behavior. But real faith is not transactional, predictable, or dependent on God's answers. Real faith doesn't put God in a box and make your prayer life all about you.

Let's be clear that God wants you to pray for yourself and bring *all* your needs to Him. He cares about the tiniest details, and if it matters to you, it matters to Him.

Whether you're stressed about grades, girl drama, or getting a date to the party, He longs for you to talk to Him. He wants you to lean on Him for comfort, wisdom, strength, and protection.

At the same time, you'll know that you're growing spiritually when your prayer life expands to include

other people—when you can look beyond yourself and start to pray for other people's hardships, such as these:

» Your friend whose parents are getting divorced
» The girl who is mean to you and needs prayers for her heart to soften
» Your dad, who is really stressed
» Your little sister, who is hard on herself
» Your grandfather, who isn't a believer
» The family down the street who just lost a child
» Your grandmother who has dementia
» A classmate who seems lonely and sad

There is no limit to what you can pray or when you should pray. Scripture says to pray without ceasing (1 Thessalonians 5:17)—this means you can have an ongoing dialogue with God.

In the morning, give thanks for a new day. Praise God for His character, goodness, and blessings. Bring your requests to Him, and wait with expectation (Psalm 5:3).

During the day, pray for guidance. Pray for help with hard conversations and for eyes that see like Jesus. When you feel disappointed or worried, thank God in advance for His plan. Admit that you feel scared or sad, but you're choosing to trust Him. Like looking at the world from an airplane window, He sees an aerial view of your life that you can't envision yet.

When you go to bed at night, ask God to forgive your sins and help you let go of resentments. Pray for the grace to do better tomorrow.

Your prayers make a difference, and while they won't change God, they will change *you*. They'll strengthen you and equip you to handle your problems. Even Jesus prayed regularly, and He shared the ultimate guide to teach us how to pray (check out the Lord's Prayer, found in Matthew 6:9–13).

God answers prayers, and while you may not get immediate answers (or the answers you want), you can trust that His presence in your life satisfies your greatest needs and fills your deepest voids.

Lord, hear the cries of my heart. When words fail me, let the Holy Spirit speak and intervene. Thank You for the power of prayer and the calm that prayer brings. Help my friends discover the power of prayer too. Amen.

Reflection Questions

1. Do you believe in the power of prayer? Name a time when God answered a prayer the way you hoped—and a time when He didn't. What did you learn each time?

2. Do you pray with hope and anticipation? Or do you struggle to believe that God is good and has a good plan for your life?

_____

_____

_____

3. Have you ever wondered if a blessing in your life (like a new friendship or a smooth surgery) resulted from someone's prayers for you? How can this thought inspire you to pray for others?

_____

_____

_____

_____

A FINAL THOUGHT

God answers prayers, but He can't answer prayers that you don't pray. Sometimes, it's what happens inside of you as you surrender to Him that leads to the best revelations. Trust the process, even as you wait and wonder, and know that God works all things together for good for those who love Him (Romans 8:28). In His perfect timing, your prayers will be answered.

Social Media

You say, "I am allowed to do anything"—
but not everything is good for you. You
say, "I am allowed to do anything"—
but not everything is beneficial.

1 Corinthians 10:23

While touring a college campus with my daughter, I noticed many students walking around wearing earbuds.

There's nothing wrong with earbuds, of course. I love to wear mine too. I listen to podcasts as I exercise, do laundry, and run errands.

But what hit me on this tour was how technology keeps expanding into our personal lives. With each innovation, we dive deeper into our private worlds.

Rather than smile and chat as they walk to class, students simply retreat into their phones. Rather than strike up a conversation while waiting in line for a cappuccino, they scroll through social media.

How many new friendships have they missed?

How many conversations never started because everyone was distracted?

The best interactions are often random encounters. They connect us, engage us, and add a fun twist to the day. Yet we're losing opportunities for letting random encounters happen. We're choosing technology over people—and feeling lonely and disconnected as a result.

Now, I'm not declaring that all technology is evil. Like many things in life, it depends on how you use it, and I've benefitted tremendously from technology as a writer in the digital age.

After my first article went viral on social media, I was offered a book deal. As my following has grown, I've been invited to speak across the country. Even this book you're holding might not have existed if it weren't for online connections. I've met so many amazing people who inspire me and make me better.

But the truth is, technology has a dark side too.

Besides the obvious dangers of online predators and graphic content, a lot of research has emerged on the toxic impact of social media on the mental health of teen girls.

Instagram and TikTok can especially mess with your mind. As image-based platforms, they draw you into a dangerous spiral of negative social comparisons.

This presents a major problem if you already struggle with anxiety, depression, body image, or an eating disorder. In fact,

Instagram's goal is to make you spend more time online. How do they do that? By serving you content that makes you feel strong negative emotions and compels you to create ideals for yourself that you simply can't reach. The longer you stay on the app, the more profitable it is to Instagram's business model as they can charge higher ad rates.[1]

Consider *your* relationship with social media. Do you set healthy boundaries with it, or has it become a toxic part of your life? If you aren't sure, take a moment to answer these questions:

> » Do you log off feeling better about yourself and your life? Or do you generally feel worse?
> » Do you grow more critical and discontented with your body, your family, or your friends when they don't match up to the images and videos you see?
> » Are you emotionally ready for social media? Can you handle tricky emotions like jealousy when you see a party you weren't invited to?
> » Do you ever cry over a post? Do you have a hard time enjoying your trip to the beach because your friends are in the Bahamas?
> » Does social media make you narcissistic? Is your content all about you, full of selfies and your latest adventures? Do you obsess over "likes" and shares?
> » What are your goals? Do you hope to be helpful or famous? Do you just want to be an influencer who makes a lot of money?
> » Is social media a "bonus" in your life or a lifeline you can't live without?
> » Do you feel more lonely, anxious, or depressed after being online? If so, what does that say about technology's impact on you?

Social media can be a fun way to connect, but don't mistake it for real life. Don't consider it a viable substitute for the relationships you *really* need.

I know it can feel safer to live behind a screen, especially if you've been hurt, but when you give up real-life relationships, you also give up the joy that comes from laughing together, sharing stories and secrets, and hanging out with positive people. You give up smiles, hugs, and personal touch.

So enjoy social media, but use it in moderation. Let yourself scroll for half an hour—and then take a walk with a friend. Notice how much more relaxed you feel when you choose to unplug. And if unplugging causes you great anxiety instead, ask your parents for help. You may be struggling with an addiction and need stricter boundaries.

Even your best days online can't compare to the joy of real-life moments. Even if you have a post go viral, it's still a temporary high. You will be yesterday's news in a week, replaced by a new viral sensation and desperately trying to go viral again. It's not as glamorous as you might think—or as monumental as it feels today.

Twenty years from now, you'll never say that your favorite memory came from making a YouTube video or scrolling online all day alone in your room.

What *will* be your favorite memory is a meaningful moment with a real-life person. Whether that's a deep conversation with friends or a random encounter as you wait for coffee, these are the moments worth seeking. This is the world you want to spend more time in.

Lord, make me wise with social media. Help me set healthy boundaries and habits. When it feels like too much, give me the strength to take breaks. Prompt me to engage in real life and have more meaningful conversations. Amen.

Reflection Questions

1. Think back to when you were a child and none of your friends had cell phones or social media. What do you miss about that time? What changes did technology bring?

_____

_____

_____

_____

_____

2. Do you believe technology can be used for good? Why or why not?

_____

_____

_____

_____

_____

81

3. Name a time when you felt happy but then you saw a post online that ruined your day. On a scale of one to ten, how much power does social media hold over your emotions? How can you take that power back?

_____

_____

_____

_____

_____

_____

_____

A FINAL THOUGHT

Like any new tool, social media can be used for good or for harm. It can help people or hurt people, build them up or tear them down. Enjoy this tool if you have it, but keep it in perspective. Make choices that are good for you and others. For instance, if you know you'll be jealous of your friends as they take amazing summer vacations, consider deleting the app for a month or for a few weeks. See it as a sign of maturity, not weakness, when you set limits that protect your well-being and mental health.

Envy & Comparison

Love is patient, love is kind. It does not
envy, it does not boast, it is not proud.

1 Corinthians 13:4 NIV

One of my best friendships almost didn't happen because I was intimidated by the prettiest girl in the room.

I met Mary Alice at a party one night, and I quickly jumped to conclusions. She was so striking that I assumed she must be full of herself, and she was surrounded by her hometown friends.

Since I was new in town and trying to establish friendships

of my own, I envied her large network. I thought I'd have nothing in common with this beloved blonde.

Several weeks later our paths crossed again at a small and intimate dinner. Within thirty seconds of actually *talking* to Mary Alice, I realized I'd pegged her wrong. I immediately fell in love with her gentle spirit and sense of humor.

Little did I know, this was the friend I'd been looking for. Immediately we hit it off, and we've now been friends for twenty-five years.

I'm thankful for our lifelong friendship, yet I'm also aware that I almost missed out. I almost let envy and comparison keep me from getting to know her.

The problem in this situation wasn't Mary Alice, but rather, my insecurity toward Mary Alice. When I first saw her, it never crossed my mind that her soul might outshine her appearance and her big circle of friends. Rather than see her as a potential friend, I saw her as a potential threat.

In short, I had a heart issue that needed addressing. I had an envy problem that only God could help me admit and work through.

Sadly, envy and comparison ruin many friendships. They keep us from loving one another, cheering for one another, and appreciating one another's strengths.

God designed you to run *your* race, to be grateful and confident in His plan for you. When you take your eyes off your lane, even briefly, to sneak sideways glances at the girl next to you, it can trigger insecurity and self-doubt.

It can steal the joy and energy you need to fulfill *your* life mission.

It's common to feel confident one minute and then lose confidence the next as you compare yourself to someone else.

It doesn't matter how smart, talented, or impressive you are. You're still likely to look around, measure yourself, and be keenly aware of any girl ahead of you.

But the problem with comparison is that nobody wins. You either feel inferior or superior, and neither option builds friendships. Neither option gives you the deep connections you crave.

God created you to celebrate the girls ahead of you and help the girls behind you. **Nobody needs to lose their race so you can win yours.**

Your lane is your own, and when you focus on what you were born to do while encouraging other girls in what they were born to do, you grow confidence and camaraderie.

You also build friendships that go the distance.

Maybe you've been hurt or caught by surprise by a friend who suddenly envied *you.* Maybe she was kind while she stayed "ahead," but once you outperformed her, her competitive streak came out. You sensed deep down that she wanted you to fail. She secretly delighted in your setbacks.

You can't grow close to friends like this. These relationships never go deep. While you can love these girls and pray for them, you can't fully trust them. Their ambition is bigger than their desire for real friendship.

It helps to keep this in mind as you watch *your* friends succeed. Envy is a natural feeling, and you can't help it when it bubbles up—but you can refuse to act on it. Ask God to remove envy from your heart so you can cheer for other girls.

Otherwise, envy can turn you into someone you are not. It can grow like a weed around your heart, choking and ruining your friendships.

Knowing how to handle someone else's good news is a

crucial life skill to develop. So when jealousy creeps up, do the opposite of what you feel. Praise the person you envy rather than cut them down. Learn how to cheer on other girls. Brag on your sister who nailed the ACT (American College Test). Congratulate the winner of the school election you lost. Tell your friend she looks stunning in her new green dress.

Realize how lucky you are to have friends who inspire you to become your best self.

Your emotions will follow your motions, and as you make it a habit to celebrate others, your heart will slowly change. With time you may forget to feel jealous as you find true joy encouraging girls in the race they were born to run.

Lord, search my heart. Root out the pride that makes me compare myself and react in jealous ways. Help me feel genuine joy for my friends and celebrate their blessings. Help me create a community where girls feel supported and safe. Amen.

Reflection Questions

1. How often do you struggle with envy? What do you tell yourself when you're stuck in a jealous place?

_____

_____

_____

2. Have you been hurt by a jealous friend? If so, how did it make you feel?

_____

_____

_____

_____

_____

_____

3. What hurtful remark have you made because you felt jealous? What do you wish you'd done differently?

_____

_____

_____

_____

_____

_____

_____

A FINAL THOUGHT

Every day when you wake up, you have a choice. You can compare yourself to other girls and worry about looking bad in comparison, or you can celebrate them. You can remember how you're all on the same team. It's natural to feel envy, and nobody ever masters this emotion, but reframing your perspective and not acting on knee-jerk reactions will save your relationships. It will keep your heart at peace.

Gratitude & Contentment

I know what it is to be in need, and I know what it is to have plenty. I have learned the secret of being content in any and every situation, whether well fed or hungry, whether living in plenty or in want. I can do all this through him who gives me strength.

Philippians 4:12–13 NIV

The most stressful year of my life was the year a huge oak tree fell on our home.

It happened during a storm on Labor Day weekend.

It felt like an earthquake when a backyard tree crashed into our master bedroom. We were thankful nobody was hurt, but this was a major shock. Just ten days earlier, we'd moved into this home, thrilled to have more space.

This tree felt like a punishment, a gavel of judgment that tore into our roof and destroyed our cozy haven. I wondered if God was mad at me. I wondered why He let this happen.

While epiphanies and answers never miraculously came, I can now say that year transformed me. Between this and two other scares in our family, I spent a lot of time talking to God. He changed my heart and perspective.

While our home was being renovated, we moved four times and spent nine months in a rental. We were blessed to have places to stay, but the logistics of repeatedly moving six people and keeping up with schedules was a lot to juggle. When my husband began a new job that required a commute, overseeing the home renovations fell on me. Never had I felt so overwhelmed and ill-equipped.

In the middle of this chaos and disruption, however, I learned to be grateful and content. I started to notice the beauty of nature as I struggled to find beauty in a home with boxes stacked to the ceiling.

On the outside, my life was a mess. But on the inside, I experienced a profound growth spurt that completely revamped my faith.

Each morning when I woke up, the stress of my situation hit me. I couldn't even get out of bed without first praying for help. I begged for help to survive the day, and I asked God to give me strength. On several occasions, I sensed Jesus beside me bringing calm to my soul. I felt His presence in a supernatural way, an assurance that things would be okay.

When our renovations ended almost a year later, we

moved back home. Practically overnight, my stress vanished. Life felt easier again, and I had a beautiful new haven. Yet that first morning when I woke up in my master bedroom, do you know what crossed my mind?

Nothing. Absolutely *nothing*. Gone were my prayers, my desperation, and my need to connect with God. Now that my life felt cozy again, I noticed an emptiness inside. I missed depending on Him.

I realized then how trials can fuel our faith in ways that aren't possible when life is easy. While Jesus is certainly present in our good times too, we often forget about Him when we stop feeling desperate. We get distracted by other pursuits. **Yet the best joy comes when our gratitude and contentment center on Jesus, not our circumstances.** Though the world will tell you to chase the good life, God wants you to chase the God life. He has hidden blessings in store that your eyes can't see.

There is a God-shaped hole in your heart that only He can fill, and while you can stuff earthly pleasures into that hole (a new home, new clothes, a new crush on a cute boy), that void will eventually reopen if it gets filled with anything but Him.

Only God can satisfy your deepest longings. **This is why you can feel peace when your world gets rocked — yet feel empty when your life seems perfect.** It all depends on the depth of your relationship with Him.

The tree that fell on our home helped me detach from material "stuff." It taught me to be grateful that no one was hurt rather than bitter that we were displaced. To my surprise, I didn't miss our possessions boxed up in storage. I didn't feel like we were lacking. I had my family and my faith, and they were enough.

It may require a life interruption for you to see what's

enough for you. Your blessings may need to be pared down in order for you to see your need for Jesus. If a setback helps you realize what matters most to you (like your loved ones and God), consider it a gift. The secret to a thriving faith is knowing which blessings to focus on as you face challenges every day.

Lord, prepare my heart for the highs and lows ahead. Teach me how to live unaffected in all my circumstances. Help me to detach from material "stuff" so I can cling to Jesus. Show me the hidden blessings found in stressful times. Amen.

Reflection Questions

1. Do gratitude and contentment come naturally to you? If not, how can you grow in these areas?

2. Psalm 118:24 says, "This is the day the Lᴏʀᴅ has made. We will rejoice and be glad in it." How can this verse reset your morning mindset?

_____

_____

3. What do you stuff into your God-shaped hole? What makes you feel happy, full, and satisfied until the hole reopens and you need a new pleasure?

_____

_____

_____

_____

_____

A FINAL THOUGHT

It is human nature to dwell on the negative and complain when hard times hit. But negativity left unchecked will slowly harden your heart. And a hardened heart makes it hard to see what is good and right in your life. Gratitude opens your eyes to little joys and hidden blessings. When you practice gratitude and contentment, especially in chaos, you're able to "bloom where you are planted." You can grow and flourish despite your circumstances. Even in times of misfortune, God can bring you calm. You can feel intimately close to Him.

New Beginnings

"For I am about to do something new. See, I have already begun! Do you not see it? I will make a pathway through the wilderness. I will create rivers in the dry wasteland."

Isaiah 43:19

Sometimes life will bring you more questions than answers.

Especially when you enter new territory, you may feel overwhelmed, scared, or confused. Your mind may race with worst-case scenarios.

You'll wish that you had a road map, a detailed five-year plan. While God may reveal your next step or two, He won't share your entire life plan at once.

Why? Because then you wouldn't need Him. You wouldn't have to put your trust in Him. Instead, you'd take your road map and run.

Trusting God as you start over is what my friend Annie calls "going not knowing." It requires a leap of faith as you let Him continually guide you.

One night during the week before my daughter left home, we went on a walk. Out of the blue, she expressed her fears and concerns about this new chapter of adulthood.

Up until this point, she'd felt very confident. She was ready and excited to leave home. But on the verge of her actual transition, she suddenly doubted herself. She had many rising questions.

What if I don't make friends?
What if sorority recruitment doesn't go well?
What if I can't handle life on my own?
What if, what if, what if . . . ?

These were all legitimate questions, and as I listened to her concerns, a switch inside me flipped. I realized then that my new role was to be her biggest cheerleader. To assure her that she was ready and give her a confidence boost.

"You are *so* ready!" I told her. "I wouldn't let you leave home if I didn't believe that. Just because you don't have all the answers doesn't mean you can't handle what's ahead. Making a mistake or getting lost doesn't mean you're not ready either."

I explained how this was just the beginning of many life transitions. From now on, she'd constantly be thrown into new chapters and new territory.

Just as she figured out her freshman year, she'd move into sophomore year.

Just as she graduated from college, she'd enter the working world and have a major learning curve there.

If she got married or became a mother, those stages would bring changes too, and so would her thirties, forties, and fifties. Yet through it all, God would prepare her. He'd pave the way by letting each new season build on the one before.

My daughter did great in her college transition, and I watched proudly as she found her footing. Yet our conversation from that walk made me think, *How often do we panic on the verge of change? How often do we feel unequipped? How often do we need a cheerleader to tell us we're ready to go?*

As you grow up, you'll constantly enter new territory. You'll have to leave your comfort zone and adjust to sudden change.

While some new beginnings are fun, others don't go smoothly. You may face an unpleasant season that makes you miss the past.

When this happens to you, don't ruminate on your "glory days." Don't assume your best life is over. Don't get so stuck in yearning for what you left behind that you resist a fresh start.

It's normal to get nostalgic when a new chapter feels hard. It's good to be honest and work through your emotions. But don't let romanticized memories steal the joy of today. To truly move forward, you've got to let go of your old life and anticipate what will be.

Remember these truths as you wait:

» God walks before you and with you, never leaving you (Deuteronomy 31:8).
» There is a right time for everything, a time to hold on and a time to let go (Ecclesiastes 3:1–6).
» A seed put into the ground must die before becoming a plant (1 Corinthians 15:36).

God makes everything beautiful in its time (Ecclesiastes 3:11). He blazes new paths where paths don't exist. He is cheering wildly for you, and so am I. You can handle the new beginning that is just around the corner and find new blessings in that season too.

Lord, pave the way for me. Help me be brave and anticipate what You may do. When nostalgia gets the best of me, renew my hope for the future. Keep my heart centered and my eyes looking forward. Amen.

Reflection Questions

1. How do you respond to new beginnings? Do you find them exciting, motivating, terrifying, or paralyzing? What helps you feel prepared?

2. New territory can bring a lot of uncertainty. How do you respond when your mind gets consumed with what-if scenarios?

_____

_____

3. What life transition are you preparing for now? Do you feel ready? Describe your feelings and state of mind.

_____

_____

_____

_____

_____

_____

_____

A FINAL THOUGHT

Change is inevitable, and you're probably experiencing change right now. Maybe your friend group is starting to split. Maybe your boyfriend is losing interest. Maybe your dad just got a new job, and you're being forced to move. Whatever change you're facing, don't panic and assume the worst. Don't resort to desperate measures to keep the status quo. Instead, trust God with the unknown. Ask Him to reveal your next right step as you embark on a new beginning.

Community

How good and pleasant it is when
God's people live together in unity!

Psalm 133:1 NIV

W hen my daughter was in elementary school, she
had a close group of friends.

She loved her BFFs, and while I felt thank-
ful for this, I encouraged her to notice her classmates beyond
her immediate circle.

"Not everyone has found their friends yet," I'd remind
her, "and even a smile or an encouraging word could mean the
world to someone who feels like an outsider."

At first, my words didn't sink in. My daughter felt so

happy and content with her friends that she didn't desire to make new ones. But in middle school, she began to branch out. She learned to be friendly beyond her friend group—and developed a life skill and habit that I consider essential.

I've always told my daughters to cast a wide net by being kind to everyone. It's okay to have your best friends (nobody has the time or capacity to be best friends with twenty people), but don't let that stop you from making new friends. Don't get so cozy with your favorite people that you miss opportunities to positively impact others.

I knew my advice was finally hitting home when this daughter (and her sisters) began to say things like this:

"She's my French class friend."

"She's my PE friend."

"She's my gymnastics friend."

"She's my lunchroom friend."

Having best friends is a blessing, and we all want—and need—lifelong sisters of the heart who we deeply trust. Friends who will stay in our life forever.

At the same time, we're designed to live in a bigger community too, to connect on a broader scale with the people we encounter through proximity or through a common interest, passion, or purpose.

You can build community with your dance friends. Book club friends. Theater friends. Art friends. Science friends. Young Life friends. Church friends. Track friends. The list goes on.

Even if these aren't your forever friends, they serve a purpose. They help you tap into a deeper part of yourself, a part that brings you alive. When you meet someone who shares your love for writing, for example, you go from a zero to an eight on the get-to-know-you scale. You feel an instant and inexplicable connection.

Throughout your life, God will continually place people on your path who are meant to help you, inspire you, motivate you, teach you, and stretch you. They may be your age, older, or younger. A new acquaintance today could become your best friend or best ally down the road, and you never know how God will weave your stories together or bring someone back into your life in a pivotal way.

Sadly, many girls miss these connections by staying singularly focused on their best friends. Like my daughter in elementary school, they assume that what they have is good enough. By never branching out, they paint themselves into a corner. They forget that God created us to take care of all our sisters and brothers and create unity wherever possible.

Rather than cast a wide net and open their hearts to new friends, they stay in cliques. Some cliques get so tight they operate like gangs: no one gets in, no one gets out, and no one disobeys the leader. Mingling with outsiders is forbidden.

And when drama blows up (which inevitably happens) these girls have nowhere to go. Nobody will take them in because they acted so exclusively.

But if you've cast a wide net, you'll have options. You won't be forced to stay in unhealthy situations that don't allow room for personal growth. You'll have other communities you can lean on as the dust settles.

On a good day, having many friends in different places is a bonus. On a bad day, it's a lifeline.

I believe it's important to treat everyone like a friend until they give you a good reason not to. While it takes time to discover your forever friends, casting a wide net improves your odds of success. The more people you meet, the more likely you are to find compatibility.

Be friendly beyond your friend group by taking a genuine

interest in others. Introduce yourself in new situations. Look people in the eye. Listen intently as someone shares their story and ask good questions. This is the kind of community most people want—and the community you have the power to build.

———————————— ⊣ ⊢ ————————————

Lord, open my eyes to bigger possibilities. Help me initiate and engage in conversations with the people I see weekly. Forgive me for the times I've ignored someone because I failed to see their value or relevance to me. Teach me to build bridges that lead to community and promising new friendships. Amen.

———————————— ⊣ ⊢ ————————————

Reflection Questions

1. What does *community* mean to you? Describe one community in your life that gives you a sense of belonging.

_____

_____

_____

_____

2. Did any of your friendships start because someone branched out and talked to you? If so, how did this make you feel?

_____

_____

_____

_____

3. Does anxiety or the fear of rejection keep you from initiating conversations and building community? If so, who can help you work through these roadblocks?

_____

_____

_____

_____

A FINAL THOUGHT

Life is hard—and life feels harder without friends and community. Having the right people by your side can lighten your load and make your burdens feel more bearable. Relationships matter, and having close relationships (more so than having money or fame) will keep you happy throughout your life.[1] Learn to build community and find common ground with the people in your daily or weekly life. Even when you run in different circles, bonding over a shared interest, passion, or purpose can deeply enrich your journey.

Anxiety

Cast all your anxiety on him
because he cares for you.

1 Peter 5:7 NIV

My friend's sixteen-year-old daughter called her from school one day, panicked and stressed.

"Mom," she said, "you've got to pick me up from school! Everybody is saying how hard this history test is. I know I'll fail it. Please come get me so I don't have to take it today!"

Immediately my friend knew that her daughter had spent time in The Mall, the common area of her high school where students congregate between classes.

In The Mall, kids often freak out as they discuss their grades and tests. My friend had warned her daughter about "The Mall Mentality," and this was exactly why.

She calmly replied, "I'm not going to pick you up because you're ready for this test. Get out of The Mall and go to the library to clear your head. You've studied, and you know the material. I promise you'll do fine."

Her daughter wasn't convinced, but she listened to her mom. She made an A on that test, and two years later, this straight-A student was named a National Merit Finalist. She won a full scholarship to the college of her choice. She graduated from high school with top honors and is now an engineering major.

Clearly, she is an intelligent girl, yet even she doubted herself when outside voices got in her head. And the truth is, we all have "Malls" that make us panic. We have Malls that make us think *emotionally* rather than *rationally*.

Many of these Malls are outside voices that shake our confidence. But sometimes it's our inner Mall, that voice inside of us, that fuels our anxiety through the stories we tell ourselves.

Whether it's the Mall of Social Media, the Mall of College Applications, or the Mall of Getting a Date to Prom, they can all make you feel like an imminent disaster is just around the corner.

A counselor named Sissy Goff has written great books on anxiety, and she defined anxiety as an *overestimation* of the problem and an *underestimation* of yourself.

She said that girls who worry are some of the most conscientious, most thoughtful, and smartest girls she knows, and they worry because they care. They want to do well and often put great pressure on themselves.[1]

The good news is, the same conscientiousness, thought-fulness, and smarts that can make you prone to worry can also help you fight it. With guidance, you can replace your anxiety with healthier thoughts.

God wants you to give your anxiety to Him. He knows if you don't give it to Him, you'll try to control your life a little too much. You'll assume everything in your life depends on *you*, and this feeling can make you panic, overreact, and try to control things as your brain spins into fight-or-flight mode.

This elevates anxiety. It makes you fixate on every what-if disaster scenario or a singular vision of how your life *should* go. If Plan A doesn't work out, there is no Plan B. Life is over.

But as you play God, you forget to trust God. You focus on your limitations rather than His supernatural power. You forget that when Plan A fails, Plan B comes into play. There are twenty-five other letters in the alphabet!

This means that if you don't win the big race, get the hot date, earn the promotion, or gain acceptance in one specific group, God will create another path. He'll open the doors that need to be opened. You just need to obey and do your part.

You were created to live bravely and boldly for Jesus, but anxiety can prevent you from doing that. It makes you live feeling scared and small. So, if you have anxiety, don't just live with it. Don't let it steal your peace, joy, and confidence.

Instead, use your body's own toolbox. Practice breathing techniques to calm yourself down when anxiety starts to rise. The 4–7–8 breathing technique is my favorite one— all you do is breathe in for four seconds, hold your breath for seven seconds, and exhale for eight seconds. It really does work!

Another strategy is to replace your anxious thoughts with truths like Psalm 94:19, Psalm 112:7, Matthew 6:34, Matthew 6:26–27, and Proverbs 1:33.

You can also channel your anxiety into a creative hobby. I know one teenage girl who started making stationery to cope with anxiety, and she now has a booming art business. I smile when I see her work because I know the backstory.

Working with trusted adults to reframe your perspective of stressful situations also helps tremendously because they ground you in the facts of a situation, not your feelings. So lean on your mom, your mentor, or your counselor. Rather than focus on how big your problems are, remind yourself of how big your God is. Never underestimate what He can do.

When the "Malls" in your life make your mind start to spiral, use truth and logic to calm yourself down. Give your anxious thoughts to God. Ask Him to renew your mind and relieve you from the feeling that your entire life depends on you.

Lord, soothe my anxious heart. Take the weight of the world off my shoulders. Help me trust You with the future and follow Your plan for me. Amen.

Reflection Questions

1. Philippians 4:6 says, "Don't worry about anything; instead, pray about everything. Tell God what you need, and thank him for all he has done." What role, if any, does prayer play in your life? Do you ever feel less anxious after taking a minute to pray?

---

2. Anxiety has snowballed into a teenage epidemic. What factors do you think contribute to this? How can parents help?

---

3. Redirecting your anxiety into healthy activities can help you cope. What brings you to a place of calm? Is it art, exercise, prayer, music, time in nature, time with friends, or a gratitude journal? How can you carve out more time for it?

_____

_____

_____

_____

_____

_____

A FINAL THOUGHT

You've probably imagined catastrophes that never happened. You've pondered many what-ifs. Anxiety lives in the future, yet God is found in the present, so when your mind fixates on future worries, you miss Him. You miss seeing His hand in little things like the cookies your friend dropped off, the encouraging email from your teacher, or the rainbow over the soccer field as you practiced for the big game. These things center you, calm you, and draw you into God's presence. They remind you not to be scared, because you've given your anxiety to Someone bigger than you.

Family

Most important of all, continue to
show deep love for each other, for
love covers a multitude of sins.

1 Peter 4:8

My comparison spiral started with a Facebook video. A college friend of mine shared a clip of himself playing the guitar while his teenage daughter sang.

Her sweet voice brought tears to my eyes. Their tender relationship made me smile. They weren't putting on a show; this was a sneak peek behind the curtain of a genuinely close father-daughter relationship.

At first, I felt captivated. But then, a new feeling surfaced. I suddenly felt . . . *jealous.*

Why? Because I wanted this exact experience for my daughters. I felt like they'd been cheated by not having it.

So I started to dream up ways to make this happen.

First, my husband needed guitar lessons.

Second, my daughters needed singing lessons.

And third, I needed to convince all of them that this was a great idea.

Ten seconds into my plan, I laughed at myself. I realized the ridiculousness of this idea. While my family has many skills, musical talent is *not* one of them.

Even imagining my husband on the guitar was funny because that's not his personality. Yet in the fog of comparison, I lost sight of that.

I lost sight of his strengths and the deep bond he's built with our daughters without any help from me. From reading them bedtime stories every night when they were little to helping with math homework to cooking dinner to guiding, protecting, and providing for them in countless ways, he's a fantastic father and husband. Our family is incredibly lucky to have him.

But as I watched that video, I grew shortsighted. Rather than be happy for my friend, I made his story about *me.* I became blind to the blessings under my roof and upset that my family didn't match his family.

You've probably had some blind moments too. Either in real life or online, you've compared your family to others and felt cheated in some way. You've looked at someone else's story and made it about *you.*

It only takes seeing one post on social media to make you feel like your family isn't fun enough, cool enough, or good enough. You may even wish that you'd been born into another family.

But God matched you with your family with intention. He chose the people He wants to shape you and prepare you for your future purpose.

God created family to be a place of healing. Too often, however, family becomes a place of hurting. Some homes feel more like a war zone than a safe zone, especially when a parent or sibling has a mental illness or an addiction.

Problems arise in even the best homes, and here are some reasons why:

» Living together is hard. We're all selfish by nature and don't always think of others.
» After being on our best behavior all day, we come home tired. We let our guards down, lose our filters, and often let our family get the worst of us.
» Familiarity breeds contempt. It's easy to lose sight of the good in our loved ones.
» Family members know one another's pain points. We know where to twist the dagger and make certain comments or behaviors hurt.
» Sibling rivalry is real. Every sibling secretly wonders, *Who is Mom and Dad's favorite child? Where do I rank?*
» Any lifelong relationship has greater room for error. Over time, resentments can fester and grow.

No family is perfect, and every family has room to improve. It takes a lot of love, forgiveness, grace, and conflict resolution for a family to thrive. It takes self-awareness and humility to admit where you can do better.

Doing the right thing, even when your family members don't, grows your character and opens the door to future blessings. One day, you may have the opportunity to start your own family. You'll be able to create strong family dynamics and break bad cycles that you see now.

By adopting healthy habits and putting them into practice now, you'll be ready. You'll be better equipped to love your family well.

Rather than compete with your siblings, cheer for them. Count their successes as your own, just as you hope they'd do for you.

Give your parents grace when possible and remember they're human too. Most parents are doing the best they can with what they know at the time. Speak the truth in love when your parents do hurt you. Ask God to open their minds and hearts so you can reconcile hurts from the past.

Most importantly, bring God's goodness into your home. Perform acts of kindness, build your family up, and pray for them. Make everyone feel significant and seen.

No two families are exactly alike, and that makes comparisons unfair. Be inspired by other families, but don't try to replicate them. Instead, let God be creative. Give Him the room to build loving bonds that are true to you and your people.

Lord, thank You for my family. Fill our home with peace, patience, gentleness, love, and respect. Thank You for being a perfect Father and preparing a perfect home for all of us in heaven. Amen.

Reflection Questions

1. Do you believe family is a place of healing or hurting? Explain.

_____

_____

_____

_____

_____

_____

_____

_____

2. What is your family's strength? What is its weakness or blind spot?

_____

_____

_____

_____

_____

_____

_____

_____

_____

3. Do you desire your own family one day? What habits can you
   practice now that will help you build strong relationships in
   the future?

A FINAL THOUGHT

When it comes to your family, it helps to keep a
sense of humor. See the good, be entertained, and
let the positive outweigh the negative. Maybe your
mom is a worrywart, but she always shows up for
you. Maybe your brother tells potty jokes, but he
rescued you when your car broke down. Maybe
your uncle talks too loudly and your dad loses his
mind in traffic, but these are your people. In a
healthy family, everyone learns to love one another
despite their differences and idiosyncrasies. They
take these lessons into the real world to love others
this way too.

DAY 23

Fear

"Don't be afraid, for I am with you. Don't
be discouraged, for I am your God. I will
strengthen you and help you. I will hold
you up with my victorious right hand."

Isaiah 41:10

When I was eighteen, I had a terrible interview. Even
now as I think about it, I cringe. I want a do-over.
If I could erase that memory and pretend it never
happened, I most certainly would.

The irony is, I thought I was prepared. I was ready to *nail* this
interview. But as I sat in a circle with distinguished adults who
asked me questions about why I should be a university ambassador,

116

I panicked. My heart raced, my voice shook, and I couldn't gather my thoughts enough to articulate my qualifications.

I felt so tongue-tied and awkward that I couldn't wait to escape.

Ever the optimist, I convinced myself that maybe it wasn't as bad as I thought. Maybe the interviewers hadn't noticed my nervousness or fragmented answers. Maybe the panel could see the diamond in the rough and would grant me a second interview to redeem myself.

When the callback list was posted, I discovered that everyone I knew who'd interviewed made the cut—except for me. For the first time in my overachieving life, I wasn't even a finalist. The reality that I'd bombed this dream of mine was absolutely crushing.

This experience triggered a new fear of interviews. I stopped trusting myself and lost confidence. One bad experience did a real number on my psyche, and for several years afterward, I bombed other interviews too.

A fear of interviews became my new normal.

It wasn't until I began interviewing for jobs my senior year of college that I stopped having a visceral reaction. Having good conversations with potential employers gave me the reset I needed. I learned to relax and even enjoy the interview process.

We all have fears that shake our confidence. We have anxieties that get triggered as we stop trusting ourselves. While some fears are understandable, other fears are irrational. They don't make sense, but we get stuck in them anyway.

Sometimes it's easier to shrink back than to put yourself in a vulnerable position.

But God created you for more. He calls you to walk forward *with* your fear and *despite* your fear, always trusting Him.

The most repeated message in the Bible is "do not fear" because God knows how crippling fear can be. The only fear you need is a healthy fear of God, which is the beginning of knowledge (Proverbs 1:7). Next to that, other fears grow small in comparison.

God wants your faith to be bigger than your fear. And when your voice shakes, your knees tremble, and your mind can't gather thoughts, it helps to remember these truths:

- » God walks *with* you and *before* you. He never fails or abandons you (Deuteronomy 31:8).
- » God hasn't given you a spirit of fear but a spirit of power, love, and self-discipline (2 Timothy 1:7).
- » God's perfect love casts out fear (1 John 4:18).
- » God can free you from your fears, so pray to Him (Psalm 34:4).
- » God will fight for you; you just have to be still (Exodus 14:14).
- » God is your protector, fortress, refuge, and deliverer. With Him you are safe (Psalm 18:2).
- » God can use someone's plans to harm you to bring about something good (Genesis 50:20).
- » God knows what you need before you ask (Matthew 6:8).
- » God will lead you in a new way, down unfamiliar paths. He'll turn darkness into light and smooth out the rough places (Isaiah 42:16).

Think through some of your fears. What has messed with your psyche? What triggers new anxieties? What undermines your confidence?

Maybe you fear the future—or the past.

Maybe you fear failure.

Maybe you fear that your worst critic is right.

Maybe you fear getting replaced or pushed out.

Maybe you fear suffering.

Maybe you fear being the odd girl out.

Maybe you fear being ridiculed, forgotten, or left behind.

Maybe you fear that nothing will change or that unwanted change is coming.

Whatever has a hold on you, take it to God. Big fears, little fears, old fears, new fears—He wants them all. He longs to give you the reset you need to bravely step forward.

Lord, reveal my fears to me. Help me name them, face them, and conquer them. Thank You for protecting me, defending me, and delivering me when I feel scared. Thank You for always being present. Amen.

Reflection Questions

1. Name your three biggest fears. Do they feel minor or crippling?

2. Has a negative experience ever jump-started a new fear in you? If so, how did you work through it, or how can you work through it now?

_____

_____

_____

3. When has God delivered you from a fear? If you haven't seen this in your life yet, do you believe He can?

_____

_____

_____

A FINAL THOUGHT

Fear is a liar, and it doesn't come from God. It comes from Satan, who wants you to live with panic, worry, and dread. Why? Because then you'll play small. You'll feel so incapable and unequipped that you'll ignore and reject God's purpose for your life. You were made to bring light into a dark world, and as you overcome your fears, you inspire others to overcome their fears too. You encourage a culture of kingdom-builders where faith gets the final word.

Courage

I came to you in weakness—timid and trembling. And my message and my preaching were very plain. Rather than using clever and persuasive speeches, I relied only on the power of the Holy Spirit. I did this so you would trust not in human wisdom but in the power of God.

1 Corinthians 2:3–5

D id you know that public speaking is the number one fear most people have? In fact, many people fear public speaking more than death itself.[1]

I find this truth to be comical yet relatable. For most

121

of my life, I feared public speaking too. I became a writer because I'm far more comfortable thinking behind a computer than thinking on my feet.

But guess what happens when you publish a book? You get invited to speak! You stand before people you barely know and share your deepest thoughts.

The career I chose in order to *avoid* speaking in public eventually circled me back to it. It's an irony I didn't see coming.

At first, I struggled with this. I felt very unqualified. Like most people, I know my strengths, and public speaking never topped that list. One night in a panic, I called my dad for advice. He offered a good perspective.

"Honey, when you're speaking in front of people and you feel nervous, it's because you're thinking too much about yourself. Focus instead on your audience. Think about the girls you're trying to help and the message you came to share."

"But I'm an introvert, Dad. I'm not cut out for this," I argued.

"An introvert can become an extrovert when they do something for God."

His answer was simple yet profound. And it still helps me today. I now love my speaking events, not because I crave the limelight and being on stage, but because I enjoy what happens afterward. I'm enriched by the people I meet.

Yet I almost missed out on this major blessing in my life. I almost checked out because public speaking felt too hard.

God has stretched me outside my comfort zone, and He wants to stretch you too. He wants to give you assignments outside your wheelhouse that force you to expand your skills.

In some cases, you'll feel unqualified. You may look for an

excuse to stay in your comfort zone. But before you dismiss a nudge that seems to come from God, ask yourself, "Do I not want to do this because I'm scared or because it feels wrong?" If you're scared, then ask for help. Pray for the grace to be courageous.

Grace comes from the Holy Spirit. It is God's life in the heart of Christ followers. The Spirit that raised Jesus from the dead is the same Spirit God offers to *you*. And when you feel unqualified, you're probably thinking too much about yourself. You're relying on your strength rather than God's strength.

We witness great courage in the Bible as the Holy Spirit transformed Jesus' disciples. Before His death Jesus told them, "It is for your good that I am going away. Unless I go away, the Advocate will not come to you; but if I go, I will send him to you" (John 16:7 NIV).

In the Gospels, disciples like Peter frequently acted out of fear (after Jesus was arrested, for instance, Peter denied knowing Him three times), but in the book of Acts—which relates events that come shortly after the Gospels—a miracle happened. Acts begins after Jesus' death, resurrection, and ascension into heaven, when the disciples were scared that they would be killed as well.

As the Holy Spirit descended on the disciples, they became brave and bold for God. They began to passionately preach the gospel and grow the new church. They stayed committed even as they faced rejection, persecution, and death.

Most of us will never need that level of courage, but we will be asked to do hard things to continue what Jesus started and make disciples of all nations (Matthew 28:19-20).

Ask yourself, then, what requires courage in your life right now? What calls for action and initiative? Maybe you need

» the courage to chase a dream,
» the courage to make a phone call,
» the courage to ask for help,
» the courage to speak up,
» the courage to say yes,
» the courage to walk away,
» the courage to love again,
» the courage to take a risk, or
» the courage to do what feels impossible.

Showing courage is essential to living a life for God. It forces you to depend on Him when you feel unqualified.

Don't automatically assume that God picked the wrong girl for the job just because you feel scared. Don't assume that you'll fail every assignment outside your current wheelhouse. When God calls you, He equips you, so face your fears and trust where He leads you next.

Lord, use me and stretch me. Give me courage when it matters most, like when someone's life, well-being, or salvation is at stake. Thank You for the Holy Spirit that emboldens me and leads me. Thank You for using me to spread the hope of Jesus. Amen.

Reflection Questions

1. Where in your life do you need more courage? What steps are you taking to grow?

---

2. What is the most courageous thing you've ever done? How did you feel afterward?

---

3. Have you ever witnessed or experienced supernatural courage? Do you have a before-and-after picture of someone who acted bravely due to the power of the Holy Spirit?

A FINAL THOUGHT

Every day God calls you to notice a need in front of you and respond to it. That might mean standing up for a friend who gets wrongly accused. It might mean sharing your story of depression or an eating disorder with someone who is struggling. It might mean collecting donations to help a family who has suffered a house fire. While some acts of courage are seen, others are unseen, but they all matter. They all build your character and God's kingdom. Don't miss out because it feels safer to live small. Instead, ask the Holy Spirit to help you do hard things.

Kindness

Some people make cutting remarks, but
the words of the wise bring healing.

Proverbs 12:18

Four girls in the same friend group didn't have dates to homecoming, so they agreed to have a fun night together. They would dress up, go to dinner, and then head to the dance.

As homecoming approached, one girl checked in with the group. "Hey! What's the plan?" she asked.

Her friends informed her that they could only get a dinner reservation for three people. There wasn't room for her to join them.

There was no explanation, no apology, and no guilt for excluding her.

Understandably, this girl was devastated. To add insult to injury, her friends spent the rest of their senior year making her life miserable. She couldn't wait to leave high school and find better friends.

This sounds like a TV drama, but sadly, it is real life. It is the type of story I hear a lot in the work I do. Most pain that girls experience today isn't caused by bullies, boys, or parents—it's caused by girls inside their own friend group.

Typically, this looks like friends hurting friends. Friends ghosting friends. Friends ganging up on one girl or excluding her for entertainment. Friends being quick to cut ties and move on. Friends gossiping and talking behind one another's back. Friends stooping incredibly low and throwing someone under the bus.

Most girls long for kind friends, but kindness has become hard to find. This begs the question, Why are some people so incredibly mean?

Here's one guess: your generation is being shaped by a me-centered world. And for many girls, the main goal of their teenage years is to simply *get through them*. It's self-preservation. If someone in their group gets left out or rejected, they're just glad it isn't them.

Also, many girls care more about being popular than being kind. Can kind girls be popular too? Of course! It happens all the time. But during the teen years, many kind girls get overlooked. They may temporarily fall through the cracks while the mean girls get noticed.

But here is the bigger reality: nobody puts up with a mean girl forever. Nobody wants a friend who is intentionally cruel. As people grow up, many decide that kindness is the top quality they want in a friend. They want friends who can admit when they're wrong and not make the same mistake twice.

As a result, it's the kindhearted girls who thrive long-term. They're the ones who build deep friendships—friendships that go the distance and last thirty, forty, or fifty years.

Mean girls, on the other hand, suffer the consequences of their actions as they make the wrong person mad, face retaliation, or lose friends (and respect).

Oftentimes, leaving home and no longer being the big fish in a little sea puts mean girls in their place, especially as they meet girls who are even meaner than them.

The Bible is clear that kindness comes from God. In Galatians 5:22–23, Paul talked about the fruit of the Holy Spirit that pours out of us as Jesus works in us. The fruit includes "love, joy, peace, patience, *kindness*, goodness, faithfulness, gentleness, and self-control" (emphasis added).

God created you to be kind. And when you lean into that design, you feel peace. When you reject that design, you feel tension. This tension is your reminder to rise above the cultural norms. Kindness doesn't have to be fancy or elaborate. In fact, it's usually simple. It looks like this:

- » Remembering people's names
- » Giving sincere compliments
- » Encouraging people in their gifts
- » Being friendly beyond your friend group
- » Writing thoughtful letters to people you love
- » Dropping off sweets when your friend has a hard day
- » Aiming to bless people, not impress people
- » Noticing who feels left out and drawing them into your conversation

- » Celebrating birthdays
- » Treating the people you encounter like VIPs, whether they're your school custodian or your principal
- » Changing someone's day through a smile or word of encouragement

Twenty years from now, your classmates will remember you with either a smile on their face or a pit in their stomach. They'll most likely only have one or two core memories about either the *kindest* thing you did or the most *hurtful* thing you did. How do you hope to be remembered? What legacy are you creating?

Our world isn't very kind to girls, so be kind to one another. Be the girl—and the friend—our world needs.

———

Lord, make kindness my instinct. Help me behave in ways that I can feel proud of. Open my eyes when I hurt others so I can right my wrongs. Help me imitate Jesus. Amen.

———

Reflection Questions

1. Have you ever intentionally hurt a friend (like deliberately leaving her out)? Have you unintentionally hurt a friend (like genuinely forgetting to invite her)? Explain the difference.

2. Is kindness easier one-on-one or in a group? Do certain group dynamics make you less kind? If so, what does this say about that group? What can you do to navigate these complicated group dynamics?

3. Name three kind people you know. Are they joyful too? What is the correlation between kindness and joy?

_____

_____

_____

_____

_____

_____

_____

_____

_____

A FINAL THOUGHT

Being kind may not make you the cool girl right now, but it does set the stage for a happy future. It makes you the forever friend who kind people will want. Girls who stir up drama and play mind games instigate trouble wherever they go. They hurt themselves more than anyone else as they end up on dead-end roads. Choose kindness even when it isn't easy or popular. This will keep you at peace with yourself and God. It will attract the friends worth knowing and keeping.

Word Choices

Don't use foul or abusive language.
Let everything you say be good and
helpful, so that your words will be an
encouragement to those who hear them.

Ephesians 4:29

I'm sure you remember the most hurtful remarks ever said to you. After all, harsh words stick. They lodge deeply into your memory bank.

Comments like, "You only made the team because your dad is the coach" or, "Your body is shaped like a pear" are hard to forget.

Yet what is *easy* to forget are the remarks we make to

others. The thoughts we carelessly blurt out or the opinions we type into our phones.

Social media creates a lot of room for word hurt and error. There is no visual feedback that tells us to stop.

When talking in person, you see the hurt look on someone's face when you offend them. This social cue teaches you empathy and social graces.

But with technology, that cue is gone. Your fingers can jump ahead of your brain, and you may type remarks that you'd never say to someone's face. You can ruin relationships and reputations overnight.

But that doesn't have to be your story. You don't have to act on every thought or impulse. God cares about your word choices, and when they please Him, you become a powerful force for good.

You learn to speak kindly, avoid gossip, and listen more than you talk.

At any age, you can unleash the power of words. Remember what Paul told his protégé Timothy: "Don't let anyone think less of you because you are young. Be an example to all believers in what you say, in the way you live, in your love, your faith, and your purity" (1 Timothy 4:12).

In other words, you can be a role model. Even adults can learn from you by listening to how you speak.

Girls often get misguided in choosing the right words and finding their voice. At one extreme, some girls say exactly what they think, yet they lack tact and warmth. They have no social filter, and they struggle in relationships by being too abrasive.

At the other extreme, some girls choose kind words and build people up, yet they don't speak up when needed. When someone insults them, criticizes their friend, or takes advantage of their kindness, they shut down and feel powerless. When they eventually find their voice as grown women, their words are often bitter due to years of suppressed anger. Or they may continue to let others steamroll them.

Neither extreme is healthy. The good news is, you can be strong and kind. Honest and tactful. Assertive and congenial. Respectful when you feel safe *and* direct when you do not.

If you're asked to lead a committee that you don't have time for, you can kindly reply, "Thank you for thinking of me, but I can't add anything to my plate right now."

If your friend teases you at lunch, you can tell her later in private, "It hurt my feelings when you said that. I love you, and I don't want this to come between us. That's why I'm mentioning it now."

If a stranger asks you for help in a parking garage, and you get a funny vibe, you can tell them, "I'll find a security officer who can help you." If the stranger insists that you, and only you, can assist them, that's a big red flag. It's another clue to quickly seek shelter and talk to security.

Ask God to help you choose words that fit the situation. Learn how to use your voice for good while not letting anyone exploit your kindness.

Your word choices have the power to change someone's day. They can make people stop, listen, and reflect. Think twice before you speak, and choose language that reflects God's heart. He desires to see us all prosper and thrive.

*Lord, control what I say. Guard my lips
when I'm tempted to sin. Help me notice
social cues that tell me to stop or pivot,
and give me the humility to apologize when
my words create a wound. Amen.*

Reflection Questions

1. Your mouth will speak what your heart is full of (Luke 6:45). Do you ever speak harshly because you're hurting? If so, how can you break this cycle?

2. Has anyone ever lashed out at you in anger (through a text message or to your face)? If so, how did you feel? What mark did this leave on your relationship with that person?

3. Most interactions offer ample opportunity to use uplifting words. Sometimes, however, a situation doesn't feel safe, and you need firm words over kind words. What scenarios call for a different voice than the one you normally use? Have you ever faced this situation? Explain.

_____

_____

_____

_____

A FINAL THOUGHT

Years ago, author Joyce Heatherley wrote a book called *Balcony People*. Balcony people are the loved ones who stand on the balcony to cheer you on. They support you and energize you with healthy affirmation. At the other extreme are basement people. Basement people tear you down. They may pretend to root for you, but secretly, they hope you will fail. We all have days (or seasons of life) when we fall into the basement, but what makes balcony people different is that they want *out* of the basement. They see a critical spirit as a vice to work on, not a quality to be proud of. How you treat others determines how they treat you. If you want to attract balcony people into your life, then you must be a balcony friend to them.

Thoughts & Self-Talk

When I was a child, I spoke and thought
and reasoned as a child. But when I
grew up, I put away childish things.

1 Corinthians 13:11

When you grow up in a big family, like I did, it's easy to get lost in the shuffle.

I was the fourth child in a family of seven, and I was the quiet one. My siblings were all outgoing, and my brother was a basketball star.

There was no shortage of love, laughter, entertainment,

and people in our home. But when my parents had parties, many of their friends could never remember my name—and that bothered me.

Those who guessed at my name often called me one of my three sisters.

Really? I would think. *Am I that forgettable? What does it take to stand out around here?*

As I got older and entered high school, I found an answer to that question: achievements. The more I achieved, the more memorable I became.

Their amnesia seemed to disappear when I accomplished something special. *At last*, I thought, *I'm making a name for myself!*

My desire to stand out in a good way started me on a path where I got hooked on praise. I liked how it felt to be an achiever, to do well in school and in leadership positions. By the time I reached college, I was a classic overachiever. I set a high bar of perfection and put enormous pressure on myself.

And while it's good that I worked hard, it makes me sad when I think about where my motivation started.

Deep down, I believed I had to prove myself.

I thought my accomplishments made me special.

I placed my value in my résumé.

And I feared going back to that place of feeling unseen and unknown.

I've evolved a lot since then. Today I know I have nothing to prove. I find my worth in God. Yet sometimes I still feel the need to earn my place in this world. I know it's time to self-correct when my workaholic side comes out and I start to feel more like a robot than a human being with legitimate needs.

In these moments, when I fear that nobody will need me, notice me, or want me if I'm not helpful to them, my productive nature hurts me. I start to believe lies like, "I better keep going, even if I'm exhausted, because the more good work I produce, the more my life matters." It's embarrassing to admit this, but I share it to encourage you to be honest about the way you talk to yourself.

Is your self-talk ever unkind and untrue? What unhealthy narratives do you believe? What conversations are you having with yourself?

Maybe you're convinced that you're the black sheep of your family because you're different than everyone else.

Maybe you think that nobody likes you because your friends just dropped you.

Maybe you call yourself boring because you struggle to connect with others.

Maybe you believe that you're a disappointment because your parents are highly accomplished—and so far, you're not.

We all wrestle with personal narratives, yet here's the lesson I've learned: just because a thought comes into your mind doesn't make it true.

Uprooting the lies in your head requires a mental battle. It is a fight and a constant effort. **God can transform your mind, but you have to do your part too.**

Rather than blindly accept every thought you have, weigh them against the truth. See what really aligns. Take every thought captive and then make it obedient to Christ (2 Corinthians 10:5).

Replace a thought like "I'm a loser" with "I'm a work in progress" (Philippians 1:6).

Replace "Everyone is against me" with "If God is for me, who can be against me?" (Romans 8:31).

Replace "I'll never recover" with "I may stumble, but I won't fall. God is always holding my hand" (Psalm 37:24).

Your thoughts won't magically change on their own, because 95 percent of your thoughts are the same as the day before. According to research, 80 percent of your thoughts are negative.[1] Actively *choosing* your thoughts is the first step to renewal. It helps you break unhealthy thought patterns that formed when you were young.

Once you know better, you can think better. You can live better, love better, and choose better. Regardless of what you once believed, you can move forward with hope. You can change your life by choosing thoughts that align with God's truth.

———————— ⊢ ⊢ ————————

Lord, grant me wisdom. Interrupt narratives that aren't from You. Build my mental resilience, and give me the ability to recognize the lies in my head and replace them with truth. Amen.

———————— ⊢ ⊢ ————————

Reflection Questions

1. What family dynamics or life events shaped the way you talk to yourself *about* yourself?

_____

_____

_____

_____

2. What negative scripts do you replay in your mind? What healthy thoughts can replace them?

_____

_____

_____

_____

_____

_____

_____

_____

3. Philippians 4:8 says, "Fix your thoughts on what is true, and honorable, and right, and pure, and lovely, and admirable. Think about things that are excellent and worthy of praise." What true, honorable, right, pure, lovely, or admirable thing can you focus on today?

_____

_____

_____

_____

_____

_____

_____

_____

A FINAL THOUGHT

As you grow up, you outgrow your clothes. You clean out your closet and discard what no longer fits. This creates space for bigger and better things. It gives you room to grow. Your mental growth mimics your physical growth. With time and maturity, you'll also outgrow old mindsets and discard what no longer fits. You'll declutter your mental closet to create space for bigger and better things. There is freedom in releasing what no longer serves you well. It is exciting to make room for a new thought life that allows you to flourish and thrive.

Direction

Your word is a lamp to guide my
feet and a light for my path.

Psalm 119:105

My friend's daughter left for college feeling very sure-footed. Rooted in her faith, she was ready to be a light for Christ. She felt excited about her new adventure.

But as real life kicked in, nothing clicked for her. Not academics, not friends, not even joining the most coveted sorority on campus.

She tried to connect with her sorority sisters, and she invited a large group to her parents' beautiful home, but her effort wasn't reciprocated. In fact, during Parents' Weekend soon after, every girl she had hosted walked past her table as she sat alone with her parents.

It became clear that this was more than homesickness. This college was the wrong fit for her, and the longer she stayed, the clearer it became.

As she talked to her mom about transferring, she felt like a failure. She beat herself up for choosing "wrong."

Thankfully, her mom set the record straight. She told her daughter there was no shame in changing her mind, and she helped her find a school better suited for her.

In this new environment, she thrived. She regained her joy and confidence, and she graduated from college and law school with top honors. Today she is in an excellent place. She recently ranked in the top 1 percent of her state bar exam.

Her story is a good reminder that you're allowed to change your mind. You aren't stuck with your first decision if that decision only brings heartache.

Sometimes you need permission to turn around. You need a change of direction, a U-turn, or a completely fresh start.

While I don't advocate making big moves without prayer and wise counsel, I do want to free you from thinking there is no recourse. It isn't a waste of your time to go back to the drawing board and explore a new path.

In the grand scheme of life, your direction matters more than your speed. Taking even a small step in the right direction is better than a hundred steps in the wrong one.

With every choice you make, you either move closer to God or farther away. More essential than having a five-year plan is doing the next right thing. Over time your right things add up. They take you to your destination.

As writer E. L. Doctorow once said, "Writing is like driving at night in the fog. You can only see as far as your headlights, but you can make the whole trip that way."[1] I think this theory applies to life as well.

God won't give you every answer at once, but He will illuminate your next right step. Trust in small starts and steady progress. Find peace by taking it one day at a time.

You never know at the start of a journey what that journey will entail. You can't predict the detours and roadblocks. While some rough roads are meant to be endured, other rough roads aren't meant for you. Take an exit ramp to change direction before you go too far.

When you realize that you've chosen the wrong major, the wrong job, the wrong school, or the wrong relationship, you're allowed to change your mind. You can pivot and go back to square one. There is no shame in admitting that you need a new direction. If it leads you to an excellent place, you'll be so glad you made that turn.

Lord, show me the way. Disrupt my direction when I get it wrong, and surround me with people who point me to You. Reveal the best path for me. Amen.

Reflection Questions

1. Name a time when you changed direction. What inspired your change of heart?

2. How do you know when you're headed in the right direction? What clues or road signs affirm your path?

3. Psalm 32:8 says, "I will instruct you and teach you in the way you should go; I will counsel you with my loving eye on you" (NIV). Describe a time when God guided you to a new path. What happened as you listened?

_____

_____

_____

_____

A FINAL THOUGHT

A teenager's brain is like a brand-new Ferrari. It's in peak condition to learn and be influenced, all primed and pumped and fully revved up—but unsure where to go.[2] According to Dr. Frances Jensen, author of *The Teenage Brain*, teenagers can do amazing things when headed in the right direction. As a teenager, you can outperform and outpace adults. But if you turn in the wrong direction, you can quickly encounter danger and compromise your future. You can get on the wrong track fast. Rather than live in fear of making wrong turns, seek wise counsel. Have mentors who steer you well (e.g., family members, church leaders, older friends who you admire) and are always happy that you asked for help.

Waiting

"But as for you, be strong and courageous,
for your work will be rewarded."

2 Chronicles 15:7

It took me seven years to become a published author. My big break finally came from social media, which didn't exist when I started writing. But when a blog post I wrote for teenage girls went viral, it caught the attention of a publisher.

That publisher expressed interest in creating a book.

Before that big break, I wrote three novels. I cried and cried as I racked up rejections from countless publishing houses.

I wondered, *Why did God give me the passion to write but*

not an audience to write for? What is the point of making me wait? Can't He see it feels like torture?

Looking back, I'm thankful for my wait. It forced me to persist, toughen up, and build my skills as a writer.

I also understand that those three novels weren't ready for publication. I'm glad they're still sitting on my computer—not roaming out in the wild as subpar work.

In hindsight, I see God's graciousness. My writing needed more development, and so did my heart.

During my seven-year wait, I had a spiritual growth spurt. I faced challenges that deepened my faith and impacted *what* I wrote.

Rather than just wanting to entertain readers, I grew a desire to encourage readers. I wanted to talk about God. What happened to me while I was waiting was more important than what I was waiting for. That is clear to me now.

When my publisher called to confirm the book deal, it was an unforgettable moment. For seven years I'd dreamed of this call, and I still remember where I was driving down the road.

That night I took my daughter to a Rascal Flatts concert. To my surprise, this unbelievable day (when my dream came true!) was about to get even better.

My daughter and I had the best time laughing, dancing, and singing along. And what hit me during the concert was how *this* was the highlight of my day. Enjoying my daughter was the ultimate prize—and that book deal couldn't remotely compare.

But if that call had come a year earlier, I may have said *it* was the highlight of my day. Getting published had become my idol, and only when I took that idol off the pedestal could God answer the prayer in my heart.

Waiting is painful, and while some waiting periods end

the way we want, others do not. They can look completely different from what we expected.

In the Bible, Moses spent *forty years* leading the Israelites through the wilderness. He endured a lot as his people grumbled, rebelled, and rejected God on their way to the promised land.

When they arrived at the promised land, Moses couldn't even go in. He had disobeyed God, and despite four decades of faithfulness, his entry was revoked. God allowed Moses to view the land from a mountaintop. Soon after this, Moses died (Deuteronomy 32:48–52).

Now, I can't speak for Moses, but if I'd spent forty years working toward a place I couldn't enter, I'd be very upset.

But what Moses probably understood was that even the promised land was a temporary pleasure on earth. The best prize would come in heaven, through the eternal joy of seeing God and hearing Him say, "Well done, good and faithful servant!"

That is the goal we work toward. That is what gives meaning to our waiting periods.

Whatever you're waiting for now, whatever has you crying into your pillow, my heart goes out to you.

Whether you're waiting for a break, a cure, an answer, a boyfriend, a group of friends, an invitation, a test result, an offer, a purpose, or a light at the end of the tunnel, it will test your patience. It might make you doubt yourself and God.

But remember: nobody's life is all mountaintop moments. We spend most of our time in the messy middle, navigating the wilderness. What happens to you as you wait on God matters more than what you're waiting for. You might be surprised by what you learn in your seasons of waiting—and what God can do with those lessons once you get to the other side.

Lord, help me persevere. Give me a second wind when I want to quit. Remind me of the goal I'm working toward, the prize of one day hearing You say, "Well done, good and faithful servant." Amen.

Reflection Questions

1. Have you ever had a waiting period that felt like torture? If so, describe it.

_____

_____

_____

_____

_____

2. What have you learned from your seasons of waiting? What good emerged?

_____

_____

_____

_____

_____

3. Name a mountaintop moment in your life. Did it live up to your expectations? Was the long wait worth that exhilarating moment?

_____

_____

_____

_____

_____

A FINAL THOUGHT

Delayed gratification can feel countercultural in an age when waiting is rare. When you're hungry, you can order food to be delivered. When you need a ride, you can call a ride share. When you want pictures, you can snap them with your phone. Convenience is great, but always getting what you want when you want it can make waiting on God feel foreign and impossible. One month can feel like one year. Rather than discount your seasons of waiting, make peace with them. Anticipate what God may do in your messy middle as you trek toward the mountaintops. God is good to those who wait for Him (Lamentations 3:25). He'll renew your strength so you can run and not grow weary, walk and not be faint (Isaiah 40:31).

Humility

"He must become greater;
I must become less."

John 3:30 NIV

When I was growing up, I knew I had a famous father, but it wasn't because he told me.

I knew it because *other people* told me.

My dad was a gifted athlete. He set basketball records at the University of Alabama and then played professional baseball for the Cleveland Indians (now the Cleveland Guardians) until an eye injury compelled him to quit.

Rarely, however, did he mention his glory days or relish in the past. He only shared his athletic stories if they related to the struggles we were facing.

I remember him saying, "If you're good enough, you don't have to brag on yourself, because other people will brag for you," and he lived by this advice. He modeled humility before I knew what humility was.

Looking back, I see how my dad's faith made humility possible. **When you worship the Creator of the universe, you naturally feel small in comparison.** You shrink into your rightful place.

God wants us to feel special—but not more special than anyone else.

He wants us to shine—but only so that we point people to Him.

He writes us into a magnificent story—but not as the main attraction.

He tells us that our name matters—but the name above all names is Jesus (Philippians 2:9).

What keeps us from being humble is pride. And according to Proverbs 16:18, pride comes before a fall.

Pride also diminishes our ability to see, hear, and know God because grace is given to those who are humble (James 4:6). Pride makes us elevate ourselves and look down on others. Most detrimentally, pride darkens our hearts. As Saint Augustine said, "It was pride that changed angels into devils; it is humility that makes men as angels."[10]

In the teenage years, pride can look like a girl who brags about her shopping sprees and mocks anyone who can't afford designer clothes. It can look like a guy who breaks his high school's football records and thinks he is God's gift to the world.

But circumstances can change overnight. If that girl's family makes a bad investment, her shopping sprees are over. If that football star has a terrible injury, his career is over too. Life can quickly collapse when pride is our foundation.

Thankfully, Jesus is the epitome of a humble man. He is a King who was born in a stable and lived a quiet life for thirty years. His public ministry lasted only three years, and He humbled Himself by being obedient to the point of death (Philippians 2:8).

Yet two thousand years later, we still worship Him. He is still the Light of the World. He still has staying power.

We all have moments in life when we believe that we're a big deal. We buy into the hype we hear or the hype we try to create. Yet we all sin and fall short of God's glory. Next to Him, we'll always be small.

Even if you experience your own glory days, don't let them go to your head. Don't let pride distort your view. There are no autograph lines in heaven, no celebrities like you see on earth. So enjoy the success that comes your way, but keep it in perspective. Spend time with humble people, study the way of Jesus, and fix your eyes on your Creator, who can help you keep your pride in check.

Lord, help me live unaffected by my life circumstances. Uproot any pride that gets in the way. Keep me humble, grateful, and in awe of You. Help me remember the Name above all names. Amen.

Reflection Questions

1. Name a humble person you know. How do you feel in their presence?

_____

_____

_____

_____

_____

_____

_____

2. Describe a time when pride got the best of you. What led you to feel superior to someone or made you try to impress them?

_____

_____

_____

_____

_____

_____

_____

_____

3. Matthew 23:12 says, "Whoever exalts himself will be humbled, and whoever humbles himself will be exalted" (ESV). What does this mean to you?

_____

_____

_____

_____

_____

_____

_____

_____

_____

_____

A FINAL THOUGHT

Humility is rare, yet even in His final hours, Jesus modeled it. He humbled Himself by washing the feet of His disciples at the Last Supper. How do you model humility in your life? How do you serve others in a world that loves to boast and be served? You never know who may be impacted by your humility. You never know who may be watching and learning from you.

Grace

I want to do what is good, but I don't. I don't want to do what is wrong, but I do it anyway.

Romans 7:19

Counselors often talk about the regret they witness in their office. They see so many girls and young women who struggle to forgive themselves for mistakes they made in the past.

Whether they did something regrettable with a boy, at a party, on social media, or during a spring break trip that made them headline news at school, they believe they're damaged goods.

They don't believe they deserve a "good life" because they're no longer a "good girl."

159

While we serve a very forgiving God, our world can be anything but. Even in Christian circles, shame can be amplified by other believers we encounter, people who expect others to be perfect. If you're not perfect, they say, your future is doomed. You've blown your one and only chance.

But real Christianity isn't about always being perfect; it's about *transformation* **and accepting Christ's invitation to change.** The Greek word for *sin* means "to miss the mark," and that's the perfect mark set by Jesus.[1] The goal is to be like Jesus—yet even on your best days, you'll miss the mark in some way and fall short of that perfect standard.

Thankfully, Jesus came to save us as sinners, not saints. His grace is bigger than any mistake we make. And until our last breath on earth, we'll be a work in progress. We're called to grow, evolve, and aspire to be like Him.

Even on the cross, Jesus forgave the criminal crucified next to Him who repented before his death. Jesus assured him that he'd see Him in paradise (Luke 23:43).

Throughout the Bible, God showed mercy to sinners and still used them in big ways. King David, who God called "a man after my own heart," once committed adultery and murder (1 Samuel 13:14; 2 Samuel 11).

Mary Magdalene was the first person to witness the risen Christ, yet tradition says that she lived an immoral lifestyle before she met Jesus—and He cast seven demons out of her (Mark 16:9; John 20:16–18).

Jesus chose Peter as the first leader of His church, even though Peter made many mistakes and denied knowing Jesus three times (Matthew 16:13–20; Luke 22:54–62).

The common thread in each story is repentance. David, Mary Magdalene, and Peter all felt convicted over what they'd done, and they brought that remorse to Jesus, who forgave them. Jesus offers us this same forgiveness so we can reconcile with a merciful God.

God's kindness when you least expect it or deserve it is meant to turn you away from sin (Romans 2:4). His grace in your rock-bottom moments convicts you in life-changing ways.

When you're tempted to beat yourself up, keep the big picture in mind. Cling to anchoring truths like these:

» Who you're becoming today matters more than who you've been in the past.
» God's mercies are new each morning (Lamentations 3:22–23). Regardless of yesterday's mistakes, today can be a different story.
» God can redeem the mistakes you confess. Own up to them, apologize, accept the consequences, and pray for God to bring good from your sin.
» Your worth is found in your Maker, not the rumor mill. Some people will never let you forget your mistakes, but ultimately, their opinions don't matter. God gets the final say.

Many girls stay on a destructive path because they think it's too late to change. They glorify a lifestyle they know is wrong because it feels too hard to reverse the pattern, and they hesitate to bring their baggage to God and have to face some difficult truths.

But God wants to free you of your heavy load. Rather than dwell in shame, regret, and self-condemnation, give it all to Him. Ask for forgiveness. Then receive the grace that lets you turn the page and live as a girl who is fully forgiven.

*Lord, thank You for the gift of grace. Open
my heart to the grace You want to give me.
When someone is struggling with their sense
of worth, give me the words to help them.
Equip me to speak Your truth. Amen.*

Reflection Questions

1. What does *grace* mean to you?

_____

_____

_____

_____

_____

2. Name a time when you were shown grace. How did it change
   you to receive love, help, or forgiveness that you didn't
   deserve?

_____

_____

_____

_____

_____

3. The apostle Paul said that as sin increases, God's grace increases too (Romans 5:20). How might this truth bring hope to someone who has made a catastrophic mistake?

_____

_____

_____

_____

_____

_____

_____

A FINAL THOUGHT

Every day, you need God's grace, and your friends do too. Talk openly and bravely about grace through faith. Encourage those who are lost, confused, or thinking it's too late for them because they are "damaged goods." Don't let anyone believe they're a lost cause. Instead, share the good news. Remind them that it is never too late to turn a new leaf or become a new creation through Christ. Jesus came for everyone, to forgive us and offer eternal life. It was the ultimate sacrifice and act of love. It is a grace we can never repay.

Forgiveness

Make allowance for each other's
faults, and forgive anyone who offends
you. Remember, the Lord forgave
you, so you must forgive others.

Colossians 3:13

A young woman recalled being bullied by mean girls
in elementary school.

Years later, in her twenties, she ran into one of
those mean girls, who was a hostess at a restaurant. When
this hostess saw her childhood victim walk into the room,
she burst into tears. She deeply regretted her past behavior as
memories got triggered.

She apologized, admitting how sorry she was for treating this girl so poorly. It weighed heavy on her heart. In response, this young woman forgave her and wished her God's best.

This young woman now says, "Sometimes people change. Sometimes they don't. Just remember that you are not *their* version of you. Be yourself, and if you have Christ in your heart, extend grace and love just as you've been given."

Wow. That's the kind of person I like to know—and the kind of person I aspire to be.

But sadly, forgiving others wasn't always my goal. Especially in my younger years, I didn't see the point of forgiving anyone who was clearly mean or wrong.

Why would I show mercy to someone who intentionally hurt me or a friend? Why wouldn't I delight when they hit a rough patch or when they got what they deserved? Perhaps you've felt this same way, harboring a secret desire to see your nemesis fall.

The problem with this mindset is that it hardens the heart. It leads to ill will, grudges, resentments, and only forgiving small offenses.

Over time these hard feelings bleed into other relationships. They can make us bitter and defensive, keeping us stuck in unhealthy places.

This is no way to live, and only God can save us from the hostility that grows when we let grievances infect our soul.

For most people, forgiveness doesn't come naturally. It's not our first response. God knows we need guidance, and throughout Scripture, He gives it. He says:

» As we forgive others, that's how God forgives us (Matthew 6:12–14).
» We conquer evil by doing good (Romans 12:21).

» We show the world God's way when we love our
enemies, bless those who curse us, and pray for our
persecutors (Matthew 5:44).

» Love prospers when we forgive, but dwelling on faults
separates close friends (Proverbs 17:9).

» When we aim for harmony, restoration, and peace,
God's love and peace is with us (2 Corinthians 13:11).

**Forgiveness doesn't mean that you become BFFs
with the people who hurt you. It doesn't require you
to let them into your most trusted circle.**

When someone hurts you, you need boundaries and
distance. You can wish them well without granting them intimate access to your life.

At the same time, pray for those who hurt you. Ask God
to open their eyes so they see the pain they've caused and feel
convicted to change.

After all, not everyone sees healthy relationships modeled. In some homes, it is survival of the fittest. Only the
tough ones survive, and mistakes are never admitted. You
never know what's happening behind closed doors, and for
many hurtful people, there is a correlating backstory. While
this doesn't excuse their poor behavior, it can help explain it.

All you can control are *your* choices. You can
practice forgiveness on a small level daily so that when
something big happens, you know what to do. This starts
by not getting angry at the guy who steals your parking
place, the cashier who acts rude, or the teacher who calls
you the wrong name.

You may never hear the apology that you deserve, but
you can still forgive that person. You can refuse to let their
mistake harden your heart. We're all guilty of hurting others,

and we all owe an apology or two. Bravely admit where you've gone wrong, and let your reflection inspire a greater willingness to forgive others.

Lord, teach me the art of forgiveness. Help me make amends and live at peace. Prompt me to pray for those who hurt me and set healthy boundaries. Show me what relationships are worth restoring and fighting for. Amen.

Reflection Questions

1. What apology are you waiting for? What past hurt in your life is creating tension in your heart?

2. What apology do you owe? How can you right your wrong?

3. Why are we so reluctant to apologize and forgive? How different would our world look if these habits were normalized?

_____

_____

_____

_____

_____

_____

_____

_____

A FINAL THOUGHT

Some people spend their lifetime waiting for apologies that never come. Other people want to apologize, yet they're too scared to take that step. They worry that their apology will feel awkward or be rejected. A late apology is better than no apology, even if it comes twenty or thirty years later. Trust your feelings of unease and the regrets that weigh on your heart. Ask God to help you do your part to reconcile the past. It's never too late to say you are sorry or to reply, "I forgive you." Either way, you give a gift—a gift that releases a burden and brings peace into the soul.

Joy

I remain confident of this: I will see the
goodness of the LORD in the land of the living.

Psalm 27:13 NIV

A young man in his midtwenties called his father for
advice.

He was struggling to feel happy, despite his
many blessings. On the outside he checked all the boxes—he
was smart, successful, kind, loved by his family and friends,
and rooted in his faith—but on the inside he felt empty.

His dad told him, "Son, until now your life has been all
about you. Where do *you* want to go? What do *you* want to
do? What career do *you* want? But you won't find real joy

until you shift your thinking and focus more on other people. That's where joy begins."

His father was right, and his advice got me thinking how common it is to feel empty during that transition into adulthood.

The world often tells us that joy is found externally by chasing success, accomplishments, money, vacations, luxuries, fun friends, or a cute boyfriend.

But what happens when your dreams come true? When you make the team, win the prize, take the trip, earn the scholarship, land the job, gain a huge following, or find amazing relationships?

As you may already know, it's thrilling and fulfilling to finally achieve your dream—but these highs don't last forever. They can't satisfy your deepest longing.

What happens when your euphoria fades and you still yearn for something that you can't grasp? What do you do then?

C. S. Lewis once said, "If I find in myself a desire which no experience in this world can satisfy, the most probable explanation is that I was made for another world."[1] You were made for heaven, and as a citizen of heaven, you'll always find your *greatest* joy when you bring heaven down to earth.

When you love other people as God loves you.

When you pray to be the blessing before you ask for blessings.

When you'd rather serve than be served.

And when you let the Holy Spirit do supernatural work through you.

Joy is a gift from the Holy Spirit. It's more than just an emotion or a response to your circumstances.

You can feel miserable even when your life is perfect. And you can feel joy when it doesn't make sense.

In Acts 13:52, the disciples were filled with joy and the Holy Spirit even though Paul and Barnabas had been kicked out of town. Their joy wasn't tied to the rejection or acceptance of those early church leaders—it was a joy that came from knowing God, being engaged in His work, and feeling hope for the future.

Nobody is always joyful, but you do have to fight for joy in a world that threatens to steal it. Whether it's fear, anxiety, or too much focus on yourself, there are constant distractions eclipsing your greater purpose to bring heaven down to earth.

Feeling empty is often a sign that you're paying attention. It shows that you've matured and are no longer satisfied by the false promises of this world.

Let any emptiness you feel be your wake-up call to engage in a bigger purpose. As you pour into others, God will fill you with Himself.

Lord, use me for good. Help me focus on others more than myself. Protect my joy, and let it grow deep roots. Bring people of joy and laughter into my life. Amen.

Reflection Questions

1. On a scale of one to ten, how joyful are you? What brings you joy, and what disrupts your joy?

_____

_____

_____

_____

_____

_____

2. How can you bring heaven down to earth? What God-given gifts do you possess (e.g., a gift for organization, a gift for remembering names, a gift for showing compassion) that help you love and serve others?

_____

_____

_____

_____

_____

_____

3. Have you ever felt miserable even when your life seemed perfect? Have you felt joy as you faced a trial? If so, compare your experiences.

_____

_____

_____

_____

_____

_____

A FINAL THOUGHT

It's possible to feel joy and pain together. They *can* coexist. On the same day you make the tennis team, you may learn that your grandmother has cancer. As one teacher praises you, another teacher may tear you apart. Feel your pain, but fight for your joy. Look for pockets of joy each day, like the joy of snuggling with a kitten, starting a dance party with a friend, or helping your neighbor carry groceries in. Ultimately, the joy of a Christian comes down to three key words: *He is risen!* Because of Jesus, you are promised paradise. You have a joy to sustain you, strengthen you, and anchor you through all circumstances.

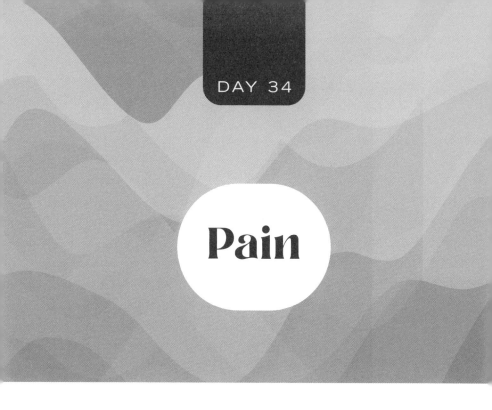

Pain

"So you have sorrow now, but I will see
you again; then you will rejoice, and
no one can rob you of that joy."

John 16:22

W hen my mother passed away, my friends showed up for me big-time.

They sent flowers, brought dinners, and checked in through texts and phone calls. One friend shipped ice cream to my home. Another group sent gift cards to our family's favorite restaurants. I felt so loved during this time of grief.

What no one could offer, however, was a cure for my loss.

One amazing friend tried to make me laugh. She took me to lunch one day and kept the conversation lighthearted, but on this particular day, I didn't want a distraction. I wanted to talk about my mom and be sad. I wasn't in the mood to laugh.

My friend didn't know this, of course, because she's not a mind reader. Nobody is, and even the best of friends can misread what we feel at times.

Have you ever experienced a moment like this? Have you ever felt like you were swimming in pain—and wished someone could give you the *perfect* thing to make you feel better?

In these moments, we have a choice: We can get mad that our friend chose the wrong response, or we can be thankful that we have friends who show up. Maybe they don't understand exactly how we feel, but they don't let us suffer alone. They give us the gift of their presence when we are hurting.

And here's an even bigger gift: God does understand how we feel. He knows every mood and emotion tossing inside you at any given moment. He doesn't need an explanation or detailed guidance on what the best response is.

He is an all-knowing, sovereign God. He's aware of every thought in your head, every feeling in your heart, and every pain in your life.

Your friends and loved ones play a huge role in helping you heal during seasons of pain. A simple act of love, affection, thoughtfulness, and generosity can be a real game changer. It can soothe and ease your grief.

Yet there is no comfort like the comfort of God, who is close to the brokenhearted. He saves those crushed in spirit and turns mourning into joy (Psalm 34:18; Psalm 30:11).

Some people, in their darkest hours, feel incredibly close to God. They don't realize that God is all they need until God is all they have, and as they get their feet back under them, they miss the intimacy that they shared in their lowest moments.

While I can't promise that you'll have this experience, I can assure you that God sees you and cares. He is present in your pain. He promises to

» comfort those who mourn (Matthew 5:4);
» bring joy after a night of weeping (Psalm 30:5);
» comfort us in our troubles so we can comfort others (2 Corinthians 1:4);
» walk through deep waters and fires with us (Isaiah 43:2);
» use suffering to produce endurance, character, and hope (Romans 5:3–4);
» restore and strengthen us after we suffer a little (1 Peter 5:10); and
» create a new order one day with no more death, sorrow, or pain (Revelation 21:4).

Our world can feel incredibly heavy. You might face problems in your life that previous generations never imagined.

It breaks my heart to hear what some young people today must navigate. The issues feel so big and unfair. But as my friend pointed out, there is another angle to this. There is an outlook that brings hope:

Bigger challenges for your generation = more opportunities for spiritual growth at a younger age.

In other words, your trials can advance your faith. They can give you a profound perspective that primes you for a lifetime of meaningful work. God never wastes pain, and if you let Him, He'll turn your pain into a purpose that could be a lifeline to those walking behind you.

Whatever pain you face, let it strengthen your faith. Let it draw you closer to God. He knows *exactly* what your heart needs today. Give Him a chance to speak and hold you close in ways that no human can.

———————————— ⊣ ⊢ ————————————

Lord, comfort me in my pain. Sustain me when I can barely hang on. Thank You for being an intuitive, perceptive, and loving God. I praise You for knowing my needs even as they continue to change. Amen.

———————————— ⊣ ⊢ ————————————

Reflection Questions

1. What is the greatest pain in your life? Have you healed from this pain, or are you still healing?

———————————————————————————

———————————————————————————

———————————————————————————

———————————————————————————

2. Do you believe that pain can bring intimacy with God? Why or why not?

———————————————————————————

———————————————————————————

_____

_____

3. What has pain taught you about showing up for those who grieve?

_____

_____

_____

_____

A FINAL THOUGHT

Some days you'll feel sad and not know why. While big grief is understandable, small grief can catch you off guard. The loss of a friendship or a dream, for instance, can trigger deep pain. Losing what you _thought_ your life would look like can also bring mourning. Go easy on yourself when you feel sad, and know that fluctuations are normal. Your life will have peaks and valleys. The crests and dips will look like a heart-rate monitor as your feelings and life events change. What you don't want is a flat line, a life of no pain and no joy because you're too numb to feel _anything_. God designed you to feel the full range of emotions. No pain lasts forever, so endure your valleys the best you can and give thanks when an upturn comes.

Obedience & Discernment

"My sheep listen to my voice; I know
them, and they follow me."

John 10:27 NIV

E very day, you get bombarded with voices. You may
have hundreds of people telling you what to do, who
to be, and how to live your life.

Social media exposes you to more voices than any other
generation in history. In one day, you may hear more sugges-
tions, sales pitches, and opinions than I heard in *one year* at
your age. If you ever feel confused about your next best step,
this is a big reason why.

As the world gets louder, God's voice gets harder to hear. He often speaks through whispers and a quiet knowing in your heart, and unless you pay attention, His whispers are easy to miss.

One sign that you are attuned to God's voice is feeling an inner tension. When your desires pull you one way and His Spirit pulls you another, you know that He's at work.

Perhaps you want to enjoy spring break with your friends, but you sense God calling you to take a mission trip with your church.

Or you long to work for a New York fashion designer, but you sense God keeping you closer to home.

Maybe you're eager to start a faith-based business, but you sense God telling you to wait.

Obeying God may mean pausing as you pray for clarity or sometimes changing direction.

In the Bible, King David wanted to build a temple for God. God told him this desire was good but that David wouldn't be the one to do it. God chose Solomon, David's son, to build that temple instead (2 Chronicles 6:7–9).

This dynamic may happen in your life too. Even when your desire is good, and your heart is in the right place, obedience may look like surrendering your plan and trusting God's plan instead.

Maybe it won't be you who gets that scholarship to help your family's finances. It's your twin sister.

It won't be you who revamps the school lunchroom. It's the incoming class president.

It won't be you who headlines the show. It's the new girl from Spain.

In these moments, your obedience gets tested. You

180

may feel tempted to tune God out—and instead trust voices that tell you what you want to hear.

But remember: Only God knows the future. Only He understands what you need *today* to be ready for *tomorrow*. What feels unfair now, like losing your chance to direct the school play, could be God saving you for a future opportunity that is crucial to your life story.

Three months from now, you might be asked to lead a community play. This role might connect you to a mentor who launches your career in performing arts.

We serve a very creative God, and you can't predict what He may do. If you listen to every voice *but* His voice, your head will spin. You'll feel overwhelmed by the tsunami of conflicting advice.

But if you listen to God, you'll find peace. You'll be able to rest even as you wait. Pray for discernment (the ability to judge well) to help you recognize God's voice. Pray to hear Him above all the distractions and noise.

A life of faith requires a long obedience in the same direction.[1] We all get off track at times, so when you do, choose the path that leads you back to God. He wants the best for you, and your future is safe in His hands.

Lord, please speak to me. Help me
discern what feelings, thoughts,
and instincts come from You.
Give me the strength to do Your
will, and reassure me as I wait for
guidance and answers. Amen.

Reflection Questions

1. Have you ever acted on a whisper or quiet knowing from God? Have you ever dismissed a nudge from God? What happened each time?

_____

_____

_____

_____

_____

_____

_____

_____

2. What dream of yours has been carried out by someone else? How did this impact your trust in God?

_____

_____

_____

_____

_____

_____

_____

3. Galatians 6:9 says, "Let's not get tired of doing what is good. At just the right time we will reap a harvest of blessing if we don't give up." What blessings do you enjoy because of your past obedience (or the past obedience of your parents or grandparents)?

_____

_____

_____

_____

_____

_____

A FINAL THOUGHT

Obedience brings wisdom. And wisdom leads to better choices. It channels your time and energy into assignments meant specifically for you. God didn't create you to be all things to all people. He didn't design you to act on every instinct you feel, every invitation you receive, or every sales pitch you hear. Spend quiet time with Him, praying about your next best step. Be intentional to avoid spreading yourself too thin and pursuing goals that aren't meant for you.

Bitterness & Disillusionment

"I will give you a new heart, and I will
put a new spirit in you. I will take out
your stony, stubborn heart and give
you a tender, responsive heart."

Ezekiel 36:26

Nobody grows bitter overnight. Typically, bitterness grows gradually. It has a snowball effect, where some catalyst or trigger event (a betrayal, a rejection, a real or perceived injustice) takes on a life of its own inside your mind. It might happen when you lose an election because the winner cheated, when your little sister tattles and gets you in trouble, when your loved one fails to show up again, when your childhood best friend spreads a lie about you, when you get excluded from a fun trip, or when the girl you brought into your friend group suddenly cuts you out.

Rather than work through your pain in healthy ways, you ruminate, seethe, and stew. The resentment builds, and before you know it, a grudge has formed.

It's been said that resentment is like drinking poison and expecting the other person to die. It hurts *you* more than the person you resent. Resentment hardens your heart—and hardens you to God's love as well.

It's rare to meet a bitter child, but you've most likely met a bitter adult. You probably know adults who stay angry at the world. Rather than presume positive intent, they assume everyone is out to get them. What spills out of them when you bump into them is not laughter and grace, but cynicism, anger, and annoyance at humankind.

The lesson for you, as an emerging young adult, is to guard your heart against bitterness. To actively combat the irritation and hate that can creep into your heart.

I'm not saying you should just get over your betrayals, trials, and trauma. Some wounds are deeply devastating, and it can take years to feel whole again. You may need help from a therapist to rebuild your confidence through tools like cognitive behavioral therapy (CBT), which corrects faulty thinking and teaches you better ways to respond to challenging life events.

When you've been hurt, give yourself the grace and space to heal. Practice self-kindness and self-compassion. Everyone heals at their own pace, and even a baby step forward is a win. Even small victories, like getting out of bed when you want to hide and disappear, are something to feel proud of.

185

Stay aware, however, that these moments present a cross-roads. They force you to make decisions that will shape your character *and* your future. At every fork in the road, you choose who you want to be and what path you'll take next. **While one path leads to health and healing, the other path leads to bitterness and destruction. While one path leads you to God, the other path leads you away.**

Choosing a bitter road may feel satisfying at first. It gives you a place to channel all the frustration inside of you. But ultimately, anger will bubble into bitterness, and when bitterness stays locked in your heart, you feel even worse. You were made for more than this, and through Christ you are a conqueror (Romans 8:37). You have supernatural help to bring good from your pain.

Bitterness is often caused by disillusionment, a feeling of disappointment as you discover that someone (or something) isn't as good as you once believed. They didn't live up to your expectations.

You assumed that you'd be basketball team captain, but then the coach chose a girl in the grade below you.

You adored your best friend, but then you learned that she just used you for your lake house.

You thought your problems would be solved once you got to college, but then you encountered a new set of problems on top of the pain of missing home.

Disillusionment will happen as you grow up and see evidence of a fallen world. We all long for utopia, but utopia doesn't exist on this side of heaven. We are *not* living in Eden—not quite yet.

In our broken world, people can surprise you in the best and the worst ways. They won't always be predictable or dependable, and some people may hurt you, wound you, reject you, and betray you. These moments are your crossroads. Will you stew in your anger and vent on social media? Or will you ask God to help you show class and take the high road?

No matter what happens, you can control your reactions, choices, and attitude. You decide which road you'll take. Real life will never live up to utopia, but it can be filled with heavenly moments. These moments are worth celebrating as you refuse to let bitterness blind you to what is always true, good, and eternal.

———————— ⊣ ⊢ ————————

Lord, help me fight the bitterness that seeks a home in my heart. Give me the grace to heal and to love others well as they heal from their wounds too. Amen.

———————— ⊣ ⊢ ————————

Reflection Questions

1. Can you recall the first time you felt bitter? What triggered it? Are you experiencing bitterness now?

2. Do you know anyone who is overcome with bitterness? What is one thing you wish you could tell them?

_____

_____

3. Think of a moment when you felt disillusioned, when a revelation or discovery made you stop seeing the world through
rose-colored glasses. How did it change you? What path did
you choose?

_____

_____

_____

_____

_____

_____

A FINAL THOUGHT

When you feel bitter, don't fight it alone. Don't let
your secret resentments grow in the dark. Instead,
expose your bitterness to light. Write about it in
your journal. Talk through it with someone wise.
Create art, or find other healthy outlets to help you
heal your wounds. Most of all, stay tender. Process
small grudges and disappointments so they don't
become overwhelming. Don't let your bitterness
snowball and harden your heart.

Talents & Gifts

God has given each of you a gift from
his great variety of spiritual gifts. Use
them well to serve one another.

1 Peter 4:10

When I married a Greek boy, I instantly aspired to
be a great cook.

After all, the Greeks are known for their
cuisine. They're adept in the kitchen, and they thrive in the
restaurant business.

When my last name became Kampakis, I longed to live
up to the hype. I wanted to cook like Harry's mom, sisters,
and aunts.

But guess what? That goal never manifested. I never morphed into a foodie. It didn't click for me, and that is why Harry is the cook in our home. If dinner was left up to me, we might eat takeout every night.

As a newlywed, I felt like a culinary failure. I envied this gift that my sisters-in-law had.

But with time, I've grown to greatly appreciate their gifts. How lucky am I to be related to so many fabulous cooks? They share their recipes, encourage me when I do cook, and model a beautiful talent for my daughters to see. We're blessed to have this gifting in the family gene pool.

I like to remember that nobody excels at everything. Nobody gets all the luck. God gives numerous talents to each of us and spreads the wealth.

I'm glad He designed it this way because 1) it keeps us humble and 2) it makes us rely on one another. If you have a gift that I need, I've *got* to depend on you. I can't be self-sufficient and pretend I don't need help.

Our natural talents exist at birth and come from God. They're inherent and genetic, shaped by our family environment. This is why two great athletes might have super-athletic kids or why a girl who sings like an angel may credit her late grandmother who sang on Broadway as the explanation for her gift.

You can use your talents to serve God or yourself. For instance, if leadership comes easily to you, you can be an encourager or a leader, depending on your goals. The more you grow in faith, the more you'll long to use your gifts for Him.

Besides natural gifts, Christians receive spiritual gifts too. When you join the body of Christ, you join the church community where Jesus is the head—and we all serve a different function like the various parts of a body that need and depend on one another.

The Bible says this about spiritual gifts:

In his grace, God has given us different gifts for doing certain things well. So if God has given you the ability to prophesy, speak out with as much faith as God has given you. If your gift is serving others, serve them well. If you are a teacher, teach well. If your gift is to encourage others, be encouraging. If it is giving, give generously. If God has given you leadership ability, take the responsibility seriously. And if you have a gift for showing kindness to others, do it gladly. (Romans 12:6–8)

It's the same Holy Spirit distributing unique gifts, yet they all serve one purpose: to glorify God.

In many cases, your natural gifts are clear. You know you have a knack for swimming, design, dance, science, communication, or cooking. Spiritual gifts, on the other hand, can be less visible and may take time to discern. Only as you experience life can gifts like wisdom, understanding, fortitude, counsel, knowledge, and fear of God slowly reveal themselves.

Whatever gifts you have, use them for good and for God's glory. Even gifts like your family, your connections, your education, your opportunities, and your unique experiences can be passed on.

If your mom gives you great advice, you can change your friend's life by passing on her insight.

If you have interview experience from a journalism class, you can coach your friends as they interview for jobs.

If you grew up memorizing Bible verses, you can speak truth over someone who is drowning in lies.

If your AP chemistry teacher made you work hard for an A, you can help others succeed in chemistry too.

It's natural to feel jealous as you compare your gifts to somebody else's. But remember, you aren't meant to be them, and they aren't meant to be you. So let your envy evolve into great admiration. Be thankful you live in an age when you can use your talents in a thousand ways and work with others to build God's kingdom.

Every talent is a gift from God. So be humble and grateful for each day that you have your talents. Spend your talents wisely, and God will bless you with even more (Matthew 25:14–30).

———————————— ⊢ ⊢ ————————————

Lord, thank You for my gifts. Help me use them and waste nothing. As I notice the strengths of other girls, remind me to celebrate them and the blessing they are to me. Amen.

———————————— ⊢ ⊢ ————————————

Reflection Questions

1. Name your three greatest talents. Which one is your favorite?

_____

_____

_____

_____

_____

2. What are your less visible gifts? Are you wise, articulate, humble, generous, thoughtful, compassionate, friendly, detailed, hospitable, helpful, organized, or something else? How do these strengths help others?

_____

_____

_____

_____

_____

_____

_____

_____

3. The expert at anything was once a beginner. Do you ever bury your talent because you want to be perfect? How can giving yourself room to be a novice help you stay brave?

_____

_____

_____

_____

_____

_____

_____

_____

A FINAL THOUGHT

Imagine a world where everyone uses their talent for good. Where we all walk as light bearers of God. How much darkness could be eliminated? How much evil could be countered? As Matthew 5:14–16 says, "You're here to be light, bringing out the God-colors in the world. God is not a secret to be kept" (MSG). So don't be afraid to shine or to fan into flames God's Spirit who lives in you. You've been uniquely gifted for this moment in time. By sharing your talents, you help your brothers and sisters and inspire them to do the same.

Confidence

God is within her, she will not fall;
God will help her at break of day.

Psalm 46:5 NIV

My daughter has a friend named Hannah who lives with quiet confidence. She is joyful, kind, and fun. She loves her friends—and they love her.

When Hannah comes to our house, she brings a white basket that includes her Bible, notes, and highlighter markers. She's only in eighth grade, yet she's on fire for the Lord. She plans to go into ministry one day.

When Hannah was in sixth grade, her dad was diagnosed with cancer. He prayed for God to use his cancer to give Hannah what he never had: a lifelong faith. Her dad is a devout Christian now, and before Hannah knew about this prayer, she felt God stir in her heart a deeper desire for Him.

Hannah's faith is contagious, and her father's prayer has benefited my daughter *and* their friend group. It will have a generational impact. But Hannah's greatest appeal is how content and comfortable she is in her own skin. She doesn't seek attention, overanalyze everyone's reaction to her, or strive to be the most popular girl in school.

Instead, she's genuine and real. She knows her worth in God—and it is magnetic. Her light and strength draw people in.

Hannah has learned early in life what many of us learn much later: real confidence comes from the Lord. It doesn't need external validation.

As you grow up in the digital age, this truth really matters. Far too many girls today base their confidence on external factors beyond their control, such as

» becoming famous on social media,
» making money as an influencer,
» getting invited to the "right" parties,
» being seen with the "right" people,
» attracting boys,
» achieving a flawless look,
» having the best wardrobe,
» winning the biggest awards, and
» building a perfect life.

The longings that girls have always had (the desire to be seen, known, and loved) can now be channeled online. The result is a culture where the internet often dictates how we feel about ourselves today.

Yet when you give people the power to build you up, you give them the power to break you down too. You put your confidence in their hands.

Thankfully, there is a better way. You can actively build your confidence by valuing yourself as a child of God. This lets you hear criticism and not be destroyed. It helps you recover from setbacks. It plants your feet on solid ground.

Confidence isn't about your belief in yourself. It's about your faith in God and what He can do through you. God created you for this exact moment in time, just like He created Queen Esther for the right time to save her people from destruction (Esther 4:14).

Your timing on this earth isn't a coincidence, and your life isn't an accident. Even if you lose confidence in yourself, you can stay confident in God. You can stand on truths like these:

- » God is with you wherever you go. Be strong, courageous, and unafraid (Joshua 1:9).
- » When the Lord is your helper, there's no need to fear people (Hebrews 13:6).
- » Those who trust in the Lord are blessed (Jeremiah 17:7).
- » God helps you when you commit everything to Him (Psalm 37:5).
- » Patient endurance and doing God's will leads to fulfilled promises (Hebrews 10:35–36).
- » When you trust in Jesus, He lives in your heart. The roots grow deep and keep you strong (Ephesians 3:17).

Confidence from God is an armor. It empowers you more than praise and accomplishments. Enjoy the external validation you hear, but don't let your confidence depend on it. Ultimately, it is your inner strength that will draw people in.

Lord, build my confidence on the right foundation. Show me the resilience that lives inside me. Use my confidence in You to empower others and create friendships where we worship You. Amen.

Reflection Questions

1. What makes you feel secure? What triggers your insecurity?

_____

_____

_____

_____

2. Do you know someone who is quietly confident? If so, what about them do you find most appealing?

_____

_____

_____

_____

3. Name a time when an external event shook your confidence. What can this teach you about finding strength in God?

_____

_____

_____

_____

_____

_____

_____

_____

A FINAL THOUGHT

To succeed in many things, you need confidence. When you take an exam, you need confidence that you'll remember what you learned. When you give a speech, you need confidence that you've prepared well and can recover if you mess up. When you walk into a party or introduce yourself, you need confidence that you are worth talking to. Confidence isn't about being arrogant, bigheaded, showy, or narcissistic. It's about being rooted in God. You feel confident because of _Him_.

DAY 39

Quiet Time & Rest

"Come to me, all who labor and are heavy laden, and I will give you rest. . . . For my yoke is easy, and my burden is light."

Matthew 11:28, 30 ESV

I don't know about you, but I always crave Chick-fil-A on Sundays.

In fact, I can't drive by a Chick-fil-A on Sunday without wanting a chicken sandwich.

If you're a Chick-fil-A fan too, then you know these restaurants are closed on Sunday to honor the Lord. It was a

200

decision that S. Truett Cathy, Chick-fil-A's founder, made due to his deep faith when he started the chain.

The Bible tells us that God created the world in six days and then rested on the seventh. He commands us to set aside a day to rest and honor Him. And S. Truett Cathy did just that.

It's been estimated that Chick-fil-A loses more than one billion dollars a year in sales through Sunday closures.[1] And yet, this ended up being a brilliant business move. Employees rejuvenate while Chick-fil-A still dominates the fast-food industry. The company earns higher revenues on the six days it *is* open because customers accept the business hours the company has set.

If you want Chick-fil-A, then you must work around its boundaries.

God created you to set boundaries too. He wants you to rest and restore yourself through time with Him.

The challenge, however, is that you live in a world of unrest. Technology has blurred the boundaries of healthy life rhythms.

Rather than get a reprieve at home, you have 24/7 demands for your time. Every ding, beep, and notification feels urgent—even when they are not. Only time with God can give you the headspace to prioritize what is important over what seems urgent.

What your friend considers urgent may not be your responsibility. Rather than let outside demands drive your schedule, you can pause and listen to God.

As Chick-fil-A has proved, you can defy a busy culture.

You can make decisions for yourself.

You can set boundaries, knowing that the people who respect them will be willing to work around them.

Rather than operate at 80 percent capacity for seven days straight, you can rest one day and operate at 100 percent capacity the other six days.

God created you to rest, and that's why the Enemy loves to stir up unrest. If he can't make you bad, he'll make you busy. He'll try to steal your peace.

Thankfully, Jesus protects your peace. He said, "I am leaving you with a gift—peace of mind and heart. And the peace I give is a gift the world cannot give. So don't be troubled or afraid" (John 14:27).

When life feels like an emergency, remember who lightens your load. Even Jesus took breaks, and since people always needed Jesus, He set boundaries around His time. He rested in times of pressure and before making big decisions.

» Before choosing the twelve disciples, He retreated to a mountaintop to pray all night (Luke 6:12–13).
» In the middle of a fierce storm with His disciples, He fell asleep on a boat (Matthew 8:24).
» After hearing about John the Baptist's death, He withdrew on a boat to grieve in a solitary place (Matthew 14:13).
» He kept the Sabbath holy (Luke 4:16).

Taking time to rest with God is essential to your health. It recalibrates your soul, amplifies His voice, and brings peace. You may sacrifice some things temporarily, but in the long run, you'll gain far more. Most importantly, you'll set healthy boundaries that protect your soul.

Lord, please help me rest. Restore me when I feel exhausted, and help me avoid burnout. Teach me healthy lifestyle rhythms so I can find peace in You. Amen.

Reflection Questions

1. Do you set apart a Sabbath day? If not, how can you change that?

2. Have you ever sacrificed something to keep the Sabbath day holy? If so, how did it go?

3. Our societal struggle to rest is proven by the many popular products that promise to help us rest. Things like weighted blankets, essential oils, melatonin tablets, and apps like Headspace are all a sign of our times. What calms you down? How do you escape a frantic life pace?

_____

_____

_____

_____

_____

A FINAL THOUGHT

Congratulations, you've almost finished this book! You're carving out time for the Lord and stepping away from busyness to be with Him. Don't lose your momentum now or sacrifice this sacred space. Instead, keep the habit going. Start a new devotional—and read your Bible too. Whether your quiet time comes in the morning, at night, or in stolen moments, it strengthens your spiritual muscles. It sets a habit of meeting with God. Isaiah 30:15 says, "Only in returning to me and resting in me will you be saved. In quietness and confidence is your strength." Let these words sink in as you sit still with Him.

Hope

Therefore, since we have such
a hope, we are very bold.

2 Corinthians 3:12 NIV

I'd just broken up with a boyfriend who I knew wasn't good for me, yet I still missed him.

I wanted to recapture our chemistry, the spark that ignited when we started dating. But that was impossible.

He was mad that I suggested a break. And if I wanted to reconcile with him, I'd have to cry, beg, and admit I was wrong, then ask him for a second chance. I refused to do that because he'd hurt me.

Despite all of this, I still wanted to be together. My friends and family were worried about me because the red flags in our relationship were clear to them, but not so much to me. When I imagined the future without him, I saw darkness.

Somehow, I'd lost hope. Hope that I'd feel happy again. Hope that life could be amazing without him. Hope that I'd bounce back and be okay.

I stayed busy to distract myself, and when my friends forced me to go out, I initially felt worse. It made me miss him even more.

But then one night, I ran into a guy I vaguely knew in college. We talked and laughed for an hour, having a fun conversation that made me forget about my worries *and* my ex-boyfriend. While this guy never mentioned a date, I went home feeling giddy and excited.

For the first time in months, I felt hope. And when I imagined the future, I saw possibility. I knew then that I'd be okay.

This night was a turning point. It's when I started to move forward and feel certain that I'd made the right choice. I was determined to get to a better place.

When my ex-boyfriend tried to rekindle things a few months later, I was able to confidently walk away. He no longer had a hold on me because I was stronger and smarter. I didn't want to go back to that dark and lonely place.

Soon after this, I started dating the guy who's now my husband, and the rest is history.

In your life journey, you'll also face unexpected events that upend your hope. You may go from being the world's biggest optimist to being discouraged as you look ahead to the future.

Heartache can cloud your thinking. Broken relationships can mess with your head. Working hard toward a goal that you fail to achieve can wreak havoc on your self-esteem.

Whatever form your heartache takes—whether it's a misunderstanding with friends, turmoil inside your family, losing a big race, a scary diagnosis, rejection from the college of your dreams, being passed over for a scholarship or job promotion—it's all valid pain. And it takes time to work through it all.

Throw in a crisis or a tragedy, and you may fall into a black pit of despair. You may even lose hope that life will ever get better.

If you feel this way, *please* seek help. Again, don't struggle alone. Don't think it makes you needy and weak to need comfort and guidance.

God created us to need one another. Relationships deepen as we borrow strength and lend our strength too. It shows maturity when you take care of yourself by seeking and accepting help. You aren't meant to do life alone.

When your hope is shaken, talk to your parents and closest friends. Spend time with uplifting people. Get a solid Christian counselor who can help you reframe your fears and translate your troubles.

The Enemy wants to isolate you so that you'll only listen to him. He wants you to believe his lies. Rather than fall prey to this, let others in. Find people who point you to the light, people who point you to Jesus.

Ultimately, all hope comes from Jesus. And all problems magnify as we minimize Him.

Jesus can meet you in your darkest place. He gives you the strength to do God's will, breaks the spell of bad relationships, and opens your eyes to a better way. If your heart is open, He can transform you from the inside out. You're never too far gone for Jesus to work a miracle.

Our culture paints a doom-and-gloom picture of what is coming next. Many popular movies and books leave us feeling depressed as they use the framework of our visible world to process sad events. They show no light at the end of the tunnel, no purpose behind the pain, no hope for the future.

If you believe that today's pain will last forever, that there is no afterlife, that suffering is as senseless as it appears, and that you'll never reclaim your prior joy, then you'll stay stuck. You'll only see darkness as you look ahead.

But through Jesus, there is light. There are promises to propel you forward:

» Hope is an anchor for the soul (Hebrews 6:19).
» Whoever believes in Jesus will have eternal life (John 3:16).
» One day, God will have the last word and redeem our suffering (Job 19:25).
» We can focus on one thing: forgetting the past and pressing forward in the race to receive the prize of heaven (Philippians 3:13–14).
» God is the Alpha and the Omega, the beginning and the end (Revelation 21:6).

Having hope makes heartache feel bearable. It reminds you to not discount the season of pain you're in. Spread your wings, explore the world, discover who you are apart from your family, and always keep a stubborn hope. Your life is a gift, and your future is bright. I can't wait to see what miracles occur as God continues His work in you!

Lord, ignite my hope. Step in boldly when it starts to fade. Thank You for the strength that keeps me afloat and the people who sustain me. Thank You for Jesus. Amen.

Reflection Questions

1. Name three things that inspire your hope. How have they helped you in hard times?

_____

_____

_____

_____

_____

_____

2. When have you felt hopeless? What restored your hope?

_____

_____

_____

_____

_____

_____

3. When you imagine your future, what do you see? Is possibility in the picture?

_____

_____

_____

_____

_____

_____

A FINAL THOUGHT

The quickest way to find hope is to look at Jesus—and the quickest way to lose hope is to look at your circumstances. In the Bible, Peter walked on water when he kept his eyes on Jesus. But when his attention shifted to the wind that was blowing against him, he felt frightened and began to sink. He was reprimanded for his lack of faith (Matthew 14:22–32). All of us are like Peter, aren't we? Instead of marveling over a miracle, the fact that we're doing the impossible, we get distracted by the wind. We feel fear and doubt, and we start to sink. Thankfully, God is patient. He helps us get up again and again. Step forward with courage, see the grace in your life, and live in hope. Thanks to Jesus, the best is yet to come!

Notes

Dedication

1. Frederick Buechner, FrederickBuechner.com, September 9, 2016, https://www.frederickbuechner.com/quote-of-the-day /2016/9/9/grace.

Day 8: Idols

1. Charles Trepany, "Is Your Teenager Narcissistic? Probably, but That's OK. Here's Why," *USA Today*, July 28, 2023, https://www.usatoday.com/story/life/health-wellness/2023/07 /20/narcissism-in-teenagers-should-parents-be-panicking-age -signs/70431241007/?gnt-cfr=1.

Day 16: Social Media

1. Karen Feldscher, "How Social Media's Toxic Content Sends Teens into 'A Dangerous Spiral,'" Harvard.edu, October 8, 2021, https://www.hsph.harvard.edu/news/features/how -social-medias-toxic-content-sends-teens-into-a-dangerous -spiral/.

Day 20: Community

1. Liz Mineo, "Good Genes Are Nice, but Joy Is Better," *Harvard Gazette*, April 11, 2017, https://news.harvard.edu /gazette/story/2017/04/over-nearly-80-years-harvard-study -has-been-showing-how-to-live-a-healthy-and-happy-life/.

Day 21: Anxiety

1. Sissy Goff, "Raising Worry-Free Girls," karikampakis.com, September 15, 2019, https://www.karikampakis.com/2019/09 /raising-worry-free-girls/.

Day 24: Courage

1. Glenn Croston, PhD, "The Thing We Fear More Than Death," *Psychology Today*, November 29, 2012, https://www .psychologytoday.com/us/blog/the-real-story-risk/201211 /the-thing-we-fear-more-death.

Day 27: Thoughts & Self-Talk

1. Prakhar Verma, "Destroy Negativity from Your Mind with This Simple Exercise," Medium.com, November 27, 2017, https://medium.com/the-mission/a-practical-hack-to-combat -negative-thoughts-in-2-minutes-or-less-cc3d1bddb3af.

Day 28: Direction

1. Nancy Groves, "E. L. Doctorow in Quotes: 15 of His Best," The Guardian, July 22, 2015, https://www.theguardian.com /books/2015/jul/22/el-doctorow-in-quotes-15-of-his-best.
2. Frances E. Jensen, *The Teenage Brain* (New York: HarperCollins, 2015), 26–27.

Day 30: Humility

1. Chris Amissah, "24 Awesome Quotes on Humility That Will Motivate You to Stay Humble," Medium.com, September 23, 2017, https://medium.com/@AwesomeWithin/24-awesome -quotes-on-humility-that-will-motivate-you-to-stay-humble -66fef6c3d6e0.

Day 31: Grace

1. *Strong's Concordance*, s.v. "266. hamartia," Bible Hub, accessed April 1, 2024, https://biblehub.com/greek/266.htm.

Day 33: Joy

1. C. S. Lewis, *Mere Christianity* (New York: HarperCollins, 1952), 136–37.

Day 35: Obedience & Discernment

1. Eugene H. Peterson, *A Long Obedience in the Same Direction* (Illinois: InterVarsity Press, 2011).

Day 39: Quiet Time & Rest

1. Douglas A. McIntyre, "Chick-fil-A Is Missing Out on More Than $1B in Sales by Closing on Sundays," Southernkitchen .com, updated July 21, 2019, https://www.southernkitchen .com/story/money/2019/07/14/chick-fil-a-fast-food-should -open-sundays-make-one-billion-sales/39666863/.

Go celebrate the life
God gave you!

XO,
Kari